Stitch & Sew

Beautifully Embroider 31 Projects

Aneela Hoey

stashBOOKS

an imprint of C&T Publishing

Publisher: Amy Marson

Creative Director: Gailen Runge

Acquisitions Editor: Roxane Cerda

Managing Editor: Liz Aneloski

Editor: Karla Menaugh

Technical Editor: Linda Johnson

Cover/Book Designer: April Mostek

Production Coordinator:
Zinnia Heinzmann

Production Editor: Jennifer Warren

Illustrator: Aneela Hoey

Photo Assistant: Mai Yong Vang

Style photography by
Lucy Glover and instructional
photography by Mai Yong Vang
of C&T Publishing, Inc., unless
otherwise noted

Published by Stash Books, an imprint of C&T Publishing, Inc., P.O. Box 1456,
Lafayette, CA 94549

Library of Congress Cataloging-in-Publication Data

Names: Hoey, Aneela, 1971- author.

Title: Stitch & sew : beautifully embroider 31 projects / Aneela Hoey.

Other titles: Stitch and sew : beautifully embroider 31 projects

Description: Lafayette, CA : C&T Publishing, Inc., 2018. | Includes bibliographical references.

Identifiers: LCCN 2017044938 | ISBN 9781617456398 (soft cover)

Subjects: LCSH: Embroidery--Patterns.

Classification: LCC TT771 .H645 2018 | DDC 746.44--dc23

LC record available at https://lccn.loc.gov/2017044938

Printed in the USA

10 9 8 7 6 5 4 3 2 1

DEDICATION

For PJ, Asha, and Ciara.

ACKNOWLEDGMENTS

Many thanks to Liz Aneloski, Roxane Cerda, Zinnia Heinzmann, and Karla Menaugh for allowing me to bring my ideas to life, keeping me on track, and answering my (many) questions throughout the writing process.

To Jennifer Jara, Yasuko Okazaki, Paula Powers, Nichole Ramirez, and Erin Sampson for your continued enthusiasm and support.

Contents

Introduction

My idea for putting together this book stems from two lines of thought that I think have the potential to work very harmoniously together.

Firstly, I want to spread the word that embroidery is fun, relaxing, and easy. Once you have learned how to make a few basic stitches, you will be equipped with all the tools you need to explore and develop your embroidery skills, and you will have the potential to come up with unlimited ideas of ways in which to stitch creatively. (In other words, the rest is just play.)

The second idea stems from both my love of embroidery and my lack of knowledge on what to do with the completed pieces once I have finished. I have a large number of beautifully stitched embroideries that live hidden away in a big red "embroidery box" in my sewing room. For the most part, I am unable to sew them into anything, as they are stitched on smallish fabric pieces in proportions that never seem to fit into any of the sewing projects I want to make.

To address this issue, my thinking is that there needs to be a plan in place before I start to stitch. Planning what to sew a finished embroidery into requires a certain amount of forward thinking in terms of fabric dimensions, embroidery placement, seam allowances, and so on.

Having spent a little time percolating this idea in my brain, I've come to the realization that there are a small handful of sewing projects that I seem to make over and over again. My default sewing projects include a drawstring pouch, clutch, flex case, small change purse, and zipper pouch. Each of these items is simple to sew yet highly useful to have around. This makes them ideal as a list of go-to patterns when thinking of items to show off my finished embroideries.

For each of these patterns, I have developed a sequence of instructions that keeps the sewing project in mind when starting the embroidery. After stitching, simply cut all the remaining pattern pieces and sew. The idea is that once you have a repertoire of patterns to turn your embroideries into you can happily stitch away—safe in the knowledge that you can sew them up into something both beautiful and useful when you're done.

Embroidery Basics

Whether you are new to embroidery or simply blowing the dust off your needles, here are a few basics to get you started.

1. Yarn-dyed metallic linen

2. Canvas

3. Chambray

4. Quilting cotton

5. Yarn-dyed linen

6. Fine-ribbed corduroy or needlecord

7. Flannel

8. Aurifil stranded cotton floss

9. Aurifil 12-weight wool thread

10. LECIEN Co.'s COSMO stranded cotton floss

11. Clover White Marking Pen (fine)

12. Clover Water-Soluble Marker (fine)

13. Prym AQUA-Trickmarker

14. Thimble

15. Needle threader

16. Fabric scissors

17. Wash-Away Stitch Stabilizer (by C&T Publishing)

18. Clover tapestry needles

19. Clover embroidery needles

20. Wood embroidery hoop

21. Plastic embroidery hoop

22. Clover 4¾˝ embroidery hoop

23. Tape

24. Dritz needle pullers

Tools and Equipment

FABRIC

Many different fabric types will work for embroidering the projects, including quilting cotton ④, yarn-dyed linen ⑤ (or yarn-dyed metallic linen ①), canvas ②, chambray ③, and fine-ribbed corduroy or needlecord ⑥. When deciding what to use, think about how you will utilize the finished item and how often you will need to wash it. Heavier weights of fabric such as linen (① and ⑤) will be your best bet for items you wish to be more durable. Projects made with lighter colors of fabric may need more frequent laundering. Think also about the look and feel of the fabric you are considering.

A fabric that possesses a natural beauty will only serve to further enhance the quality of the stitches you make on it. Consider the tactile element of the fabric combined with your thread choice and how they complement each other. Most of the projects in this book were made using Essex Yarn Dyed linen by Robert Kaufman Fabrics. I've found this fabric to be a natural winner—beautiful in its own right, a joy to stitch on, and a perfect weight for both embroidering and sewing. Try using it in combination with a pen-transferred pattern and a size 24 tapestry needle ⑱, and you will never look back!

Embroidery Basics

EMBROIDERY THREADS

Many different threads are suitable for embroidery. I prefer to use stranded cotton floss (⑧ and ⑩) and a fine wool thread ⑨. You can substitute other threads, but try to keep them to a similar thread weight (thickness) if you wish for them to have the same look. Experimenting with slightly thinner or thicker threads is fine, too, if you are looking for a different end result. In the project instructions, I have included the thread type used and have listed the colors by description. Utilize this information as much or as little as you wish. By all means, use your own preferences with regards to favorite brands, thread types, and colors.

Stranded Cotton Floss

Stranded cotton floss is usually available in skeins but also can be found as spools. I find the spools are much easier to handle, as the skeins can be prone to tangling. The floss is usually made up of six individual strands that can be separated to create a thinner floss. For all the projects in this book where I've used stranded floss, I've used the full thickness: six strands. Good-quality brands I would recommend include Aurifil's Aurifloss ⑧ and LECIEN Co.'s COSMO ⑩. Both of these brands offer a vast and dazzling array of shade choices and are colorfast. A selection of around twenty colors that appeal to you will be a good starting place. Add more options as you create and discover what you like.

Wool Thread

Wool threads create nicely textured stitches that contrast beautifully with cotton or linen fabrics. You can use them on their own or alongside stranded cotton floss to add interest to your work. Whenever I want to add textural contrast to a piece, I embroider some pattern elements using wool and other areas using stranded cotton. (See Colorwork, page 74; Plaid, page 91; and Daisy, page 104.) For embroidery, a thinner wool thread is best. I like Aurifil's 12-weight Lana Wool ⑨. The thicker wool threads that are suitable for tapestry aren't recommended for these projects, as they would give a much fuller look to the stitches and a very different end result. If you want to recreate the same fine stitch detail of the wool thread projects in this book but wish to use stranded floss instead, simply use two strands of floss instead of six.

HOOPS

You don't have to use an embroidery hoop to stitch, but I always recommend using one. It will help keep everything nicely flat and also makes it easier to hold the embroidery. A hoop is made up of two rings—the upper ring being larger than the bottom ring and having an adjustable screw fitting. You can use wooden ⑳ or plastic (㉑ and ㉒) versions depending on your preference.

Hoops are measured by their diameter. I find the 8″ size to be the most useful to have around, followed by a 5″ hoop. For instructions on how to use a hoop, see Embroidering (page 16). I give recommended hoop sizes for each of the projects, but if you wish to substitute a different size, see Using a Different-Size Hoop (page 16).

EMBROIDERY NEEDLES

Embroidery needles are widely available. They have a longer eye, making the threading of them easier. Embroidery needles are sized numerically—the higher the number, the smaller/thinner the needle. Size is a matter of personal preference; use any that feel comfortable as you embroider. A mixed pack of embroidery needles, sizes 3–9 ⑲, is a good place to start. You could also try chenille needles (a small size such as 24 is best), which have an elongated eye and a sharp point.

Tapestry Needles

Thin tapestry needles, such as size 24 ⑱, are a great choice for embroidering some fabrics such as linen. Tapestry needles work well for pen-transferred designs, but use an embroidery needle when stitching through stabilizer-transferred designs. Tapestry needles will also come in handy for the weaving elements of stitches such as Spider Web (page 29) or Weaving Stitch (page 30).

THIMBLE

If you embroider a lot or are stitching through thicker fabric, a thimble is a useful aid to prevent sore fingers. Slip it onto the tip of your index finger and use it to push the needle through the fabric as you stitch. Many types are available; I like one that is semiflexible but has a metal tip, such as the Clover Protect and Grip Thimble ⑭.

NEEDLE PULLERS

Whenever you are finding it difficult to pull your needle through thicker fabrics or the stitch stabilizer, a needle puller can be used instead of a thimble. Made from soft, flexible silicone, a needle puller helps you grip the needle as you pull it from the back of the fabric. Slip the needle puller onto the tip of either your thumb or index finger. I like Dritz LoRan needle pullers ㉔, which come as a pair of small and medium pullers; I sometimes use the medium on my thumb and the small on my index finger together.

NEEDLE THREADER ⑮

This is a useful tool when you are threading up fine threads such as 12-weight wool thread ⑨.

TOOLS FOR WORKING WITH PATTERNS

Embroidery usually begins with a pattern. For more on where to find the patterns provided for you in this book, see Using Patterns (next page). For details on how to use the patterns, see Transferring Patterns (page 14) and Positioning the Pattern (next page). There are many tools available to transfer an embroidery pattern to fabric. The following are my favorites.

Embroidery Marking Pen

Use a water-soluble embroidery marking pen for tracing designs onto fabric (page 15) and also for marking when positioning the pattern (next page). The pen marks will wash away once the embroidery has been stitched (page 17). The pens I always use are the Water-Soluble Marker by Clover ⑫ and Prym AQUA-Trickmarker ⑬. White-ink embroidery pens ⑪ are a great choice for using on darker solid fabrics, but note that these don't work on textured fabrics such as linen. When using a pen for the first time, I *always* recommend that you test it to see how well the marks wash out prior to using it on your final project. I never use pens with vanishing ink for embroidery, but I do use them for marking when sewing (see Marking Tools for Sewing, page 49).

Wash-Away Stabilizer

These letter-size stabilizer sheets are used for transferring patterns to fabric. They are water-soluble with an adhesive backing, which allows you to print the pattern onto them, peel off the paper backing, and apply them directly to your fabric. Once you complete the stitching, simply wash away the stabilizer. They are particularly handy for transferring patterns onto darker or textured fabrics such as linens, when tracing is tricky. See Printing on Stabilizer (page 15). I use C&T Publishing's Wash-Away Stitch Stabilizer ⑰.

TAPE

Use tape to secure both the pattern and fabric in place when tracing designs. The tape should be strong enough to hold everything in place but come away easily after use without leaving residue. A paper tape, washi tape, or a product such as C&T Publishing's Tear-Perfect Maker Tape ㉓ all work well.

LIGHTBOX

This is a useful tool to have around if you do a lot of embroidery and like to trace your designs onto fabric. A lightbox is a screen that lights up when switched on, meaning you can lay a design flat on top of it to trace horizontally. This is much easier than tracing a design while standing upright at a window. An advantage of this tool is that it can be used at any time of the day or night rather than just daylight hours.

> **NOTE: SCREEN-LIGHT APP**
> *If you have an iPad, you can add the Screen-Light app to your device. When opened, it turns your iPad into a makeshift lightbox, allowing you to trace designs onto your fabric.*

Stitch & Sew

Embroidery Techniques

There are many different ways to go about mastering the skill of embroidery. Here I share some of the techniques that work well for me.

USING PATTERNS

All the embroidery patterns for the projects in this book can be found at the end of each project chapter for tracing. If you prefer to print the patterns, they can be downloaded from **tinyurl.com/11296-patterns-download**. For more information about how to use the downloadable patterns, see Printing on Stabilizer (page 15).

POSITIONING THE PATTERN

I position patterns in one of two ways—measured from the top edge of the fabric and centered across the width, or centered across both the width and height (see the directions below). Each project will instruct you on which method to use.

Measured from the Top Edge

1. Fold the fabric in half by bringing the sides together and creasing along the fold using a finger presser (page 50). Unfold the fabric, and mark the center top and bottom edges with an embroidery marking pen (previous page) if necessary.

2. From the top edge of the fabric, measure and mark a horizontal line at the required distance given to you in the project. Position the top of the stitching pattern—as opposed to the top of the paper—just below this line and centered across the width, using the crease marks as a guide.

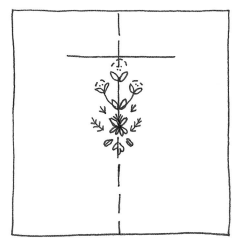

Pattern positioned from top edge

Centered

1. Fold the fabric in half lengthwise and crease along the fold using a finger presser (page 50). Unfold the fabric, and mark the center top and bottom edges with an embroidery marking pen (previous page) if necessary.

2. Fold the fabric in half widthwise and crease using a finger presser. Unfold the fabric and mark the center of the side edges, if necessary. Position the center of the pattern at the center of the fabric, using the crease marks as a guide.

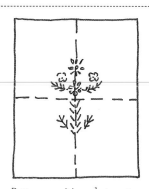

Pattern positioned at center

TRANSFERRING PATTERNS

1. Printed stabilizer pattern

2. Printed stabilizer pattern (after embroidering)

3. Traced pattern

4. Pattern traced onto stabilizer

5. Printed stabilizer patterns

6. Clover Water-Soluble Marker (fine)

7. Clover White Marking Pen (fine)

8. Prym AQUA-Trickmarker

I use two different methods for transferring patterns onto fabric: tracing and printing on stabilizer.

Tracing ③

Tracing is the traditional method, which works well when transferring designs onto light-color fabrics. Patterns are designed to be traced onto the front of your fabric using an embroidery marking pen (page 12).

1. Place the fabric over the desired pattern motif and position the pattern as described in the project instructions. Use an embroidery marking pen to trace the design onto the fabric.

2. If you find it difficult to see the pattern through the material, position the fabric on top of a printed copy of the pattern and tape it in place to secure. Tape the pattern and fabric onto a well-lit window or lightbox and trace.

3. Embroider the pattern following the marked lines.

Printing on Stabilizer ①, ②, and ⑤

This is a newer method that works well for darker or thicker fabrics that are difficult to see through, even when using a lightbox or window. The stabilizer is printed and applied to the fabric ① before being stitched ②. I used this approach when transferring my designs onto most of the yarn-dyed linens in the projects. A wash-away stitch stabilizer (page 12) is required.

The first step is to have a digital copy of the pattern on your computer (see Using Patterns, page 13). Before you actually print onto the stabilizer, check that the copy prints at the correct size. Open the printing options panel on your computer to make sure any "scale to fit paper size" option is *unchecked* before making a test print on copy paper. Inch marks are provided on each pattern page so that you can check the test copy for accuracy.

When using this method for the first time, your test print should also help you work out which way the stabilizer needs to be placed in the printer paper tray, since the design needs to print on the soft side of the sheet. Mark an X on the test sheet and lay it faceup into the printer tray. If the X ends up on the back of the printed design, you will know the front side faces down when loaded. This means you would place the stabilizer *soft side down* into the paper tray. If the X shows up on the front side of the test copy, place the stabilizer *soft side up* when loading it into the paper tray.

1. Load a sheet of the stabilizer into the paper tray of the printer. Select the page with the desired pattern, and print the page onto the stabilizer sheet.

2. Cut around the pattern motif, leaving a small margin all around.

3. Peel off the paper backing and stick the pattern motif in position: printed side up on the right side of the fabric.

4. Embroider the pattern, stitching on the printed lines through both the stabilizer and the fabric.

TIP
Pattern Traced onto Stabilizer ④

You also can combine these methods by tracing your pattern onto the wash-away stitch stabilizer instead of printing. Place the stabilizer sheet over the desired pattern motif, use an embroidery marking pen to trace the design onto the stabilizer, and follow Printing on Stabilizer, Steps 2–4 (above).

EMBROIDERING

1. Unscrew and separate the 2 rings of the embroidery hoop. Place the fabric over the smaller ring. Position the larger ring on top and tighten the screw a little.

2. Gently pull the fabric at each side so that the hooped area of fabric is perfectly taut; then tighten the screw again. Always take care not to stretch the fabric, or the finished piece will look distorted. You can use a screwdriver to tighten the screw head a little tighter if necessary.

3. Thread the needle with an 18″ length of floss or thread. Make a double knot at the end of the longest tail of floss.

4. Insert the needle into the fabric from the wrong side, and pull the needle out from the right side. Embroider the chosen stitch (see Embroidery Stitches, page 18).

5. When finished, insert the needle into the fabric and pull it out on the wrong side of the work. Insert the needle through one of the stitches on the wrong side; pull to make a small loop. Insert the needle through the loop a couple of times and pull to knot the thread close to the fabric. Weave the thread tail through some of the stitches on the wrong side. Cut away the excess.

USING A DIFFERENT-SIZE HOOP

If you don't have the recommended hoop size, you can easily substitute a hoop of a different size.

To use a smaller hoop, adjust the position of the hoop as you stitch so that you can reach all areas of the pattern.

To use a larger hoop, cut a larger piece of fabric to stitch on—at least 2″ larger in both width and length than the diameter of the hoop. Draw a rectangle or square at the center of the fabric using the original fabric cutting dimensions from the project. Position the pattern as the instructions guide: If measuring from the top edge, measure from the top edge of the *drawn* rectangle or square instead.

Fabric cut for the recommended hoop size

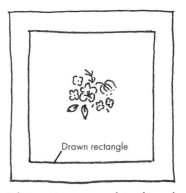

Fabric cut to accommodate a larger hoop

PREPARING EMBROIDERED FABRIC FOR SEWING

After embroidering the fabric, remove it from the hoop and wash out the pen marks or stabilizer using the following methods.

Removing Embroidery Marking-Pen Lines

1. Place the finished embroidery as flat as possible into a sink or bowl of cool water.

2. Leave for a few minutes until the pen marks disappear.

3. Lift the fabric up and shake off the excess water without scrunching or squeezing the fabric. Lay it flat onto a towel, and wrap the towel edges over the embroidery. Press gently with your hand to absorb as much water as possible.

Removing Wash-Away Stabilizer

1. Place the finished embroidery as flat as possible into a sink or bowl of slightly warm water.

2. Leave for a few minutes until most of the stabilizer dissolves away. Remove any remaining flecks of stabilizer by holding the fabric under a running tap.

3. Shake off the excess water without scrunching or squeezing the fabric. Lay it flat onto a towel, and wrap the towel edges over the embroidery. Press gently with your hand to absorb as much water as possible.

Drying and Pressing the Fabric

1. Leave the embroidered fabric flat to dry, wrapped in the towel for 5 minutes.

2. Remove the fabric from the towel. Place it right side up onto a dry folded towel and press gently with an iron, using a medium-high setting to remove any creases in the fabric.

3. Turn the fabric wrong side up and press.

TIP

To avoid flattening the stitches, either press the stitched areas very gently and swiftly or press them with the fabric wrong side up only.

4. Lay the embroidered fabric on a flat surface, and leave it to finish drying naturally.

5. Once dry, weave any loose thread ends into the stitches on the wrong side. This is especially important if you have used quilting cotton as the exterior fabric and you want to apply interfacing to the project. Loose thread ends will create visibly noticeable bumps in the finished item.

CARING FOR THE FINISHED PROJECT

Sewn embroidered items can be washed and dried with care to keep them looking good. When cleaning, bear in mind the content of both your thread and fabric, and wash accordingly. Even though floss brands are usually labeled as colorfast, I find that some colors can still be tricky and tend to bleed onto the fabric when machine washing.

For the best results, I recommend hand washing using cool water and a mild detergent. Lay the item in the soapy water and press gently without wringing or twisting. Rinse in cool water and squeeze out again. Wrap the item in a clean towel and gently squeeze to absorb the water onto the towel. Leave it to dry flat. Items can be pressed gently with an iron when dry.

TIP

To make it easier to press, insert folded-up batting inside the item to pad it out.

Embroidery Stitches

In this section, you'll find instructions for all the basic embroidery stitches used in this book. While reading through the directions, it can be helpful to have a needle and thread in hand to practice as you go. You can use a scrap of fabric to try out the stitches, or you can prepare fabric to make a page for the Embroidered Sampler Notebook (page 62) and practice on that. To prepare the fabric for stitching, see Embroidering (page 16).

TIP

Stitch length can vary depending on the pattern and personal preference. The lengths here are approximate guides, but anywhere between ⅛˝ and ¼˝ works for most stitches.

STRAIGHT STITCH

Straight Stitch is the simplest of stitches—a single stitch. It can be used on its own or grouped into various pattern formations such as a star shape or flower. When grouped, stitches can be separate from each other or overlapping.

1. Bring the needle to the front of the fabric (A); exit the fabric about ¼˝ away (B).

2. Repeat Step 1 to make as many stitches as required.

Detail of Marigold (page 133)

Detail of Embroidered Sampler Notebook (page 39)

RUNNING STITCH

Running Stitch is formed by completing several Straight Stitches in a line, with a small gap between each stitch. The finished look is of a very open stitch, which works nicely in contrast with more heavily worked stitches. Use it on either straight or curved pattern lines. The stitch length and gap length can be the same, or one can be smaller than the other for different results. For a neat finish, keep the length of both stitches and gaps consistent. See also Double Stitches (page 33).

1. Bring the needle and thread out to the front of the fabric (A).

2. Make a stitch about ¼˝ in length (B).

3. Bring the needle back out, leaving a small gap between the end of the previous stitch and the start of the next (C).

4. Repeat Steps 2 and 3, working along the pattern line until completed (D, E, and F).

Detail of In Bloom (page 73)

BACKSTITCH

This stitch is made up of a line of Straight Stitches with no gaps between them. The name refers to the way the stitches are worked—backward. Backstitches give a much bolder effect than Running Stitches and work well for straight and curved pattern lines. Keep the stitch length consistent for a neat result. *Note:* The first stitch is always worked *forward*, and all subsequent stitches are worked backward. See also Lacing (page 34).

1. Bring the needle out to the front of the fabric (A). Take a stitch about ¼″ in length (B).

2. Bring the needle back out to the front of the fabric, about ¼″ from where the previous stitch ended (C).

3. Reinsert the needle at the same point at which the previous stitch ended (D).

4. Repeat Steps 2 and 3 for the length of the pattern line (E and F).

Detail of Buttercup (page 70)

CROSS-STITCH

An embroidered Cross-Stitch is made up of two overlapping diagonal stitches. It is a very versatile stitch that can be worked in rows, repeating patterns, or as a flower center. It also has a lot of scope for variations—see Stitch Combinations (page 32), Couching Combinations (page 32), and Multicolor Stitches (page 33).

To Make a Single Cross-Stitch

1. Bring the needle out to the front of the fabric (A) and make a diagonal stitch (B).

2. Bring the needle back out at (C) and make a stitch in the opposite direction, overlapping the first (D).

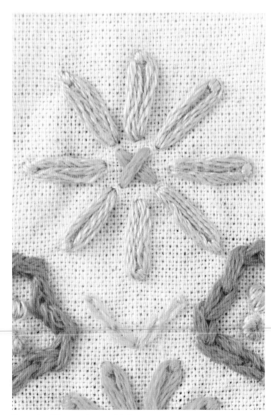

Detail of Daisy (page 104)

To Make a Row of Cross-Stitches

1. Bring the needle out to the front of the fabric (A) and make a diagonal stitch (B).

2. Repeat Step 1 to make stitches in the same direction for the length of the row (C, D, E, and F).

3. Bring the needle back out vertically above, at the top edge of the stitch line (G). Make a slanted stitch in the opposite direction of and overlapping the stitch below (H).

4. Repeat Step 3, working back along the row to the start (I, J, K, and L).

Detail of Marseille (page 131)

FERN STITCH

This decorative stitch is perfectly suited for stitching ferns or foliage. It has an open look and can be worked along straight or curved lines. Each set of three converging lines suggests two leaves and one central stem section. The instructions below describe working horizontally along a pattern line, starting at the meeting point of the first *set* of lines. The stitch can also be worked vertically or diagonally.

1. Bring the needle out to the front of the fabric (A).

2. Make a stitch ¼″ long, working backward along the pattern line (B).

3. Bring the needle back out at the previous entry point (C). Work a diagonal stitch downward to the left (D). Bring the needle back out vertically above (E), and work a diagonal stitch downward to the right (F).

4. Bring the needle out ¼″ along the pattern line (G).

5. Repeat Steps 2–4 for the required length (H, I, J, K, L, M, and N).

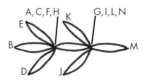

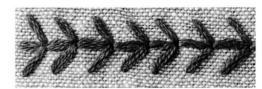

Detail of Colorwork (page 74)

SATIN STITCH

Satin Stitch is used as a filling stitch, made up of stitches worked closely together. When the stitches are worked at a slight angle, the filled area will take on a satin-like sheen. Stitches can also be worked vertically or horizontally and can be spaced a little apart for a less glossy, more open look.

1. Bring the needle out to the front of the fabric at one side of the shape to be stitched (A).

2. Work a slanted (or straight) stitch across the shape to the opposite side (B).

3. Bring the needle back out to the front of the embroidery, right next to the start of the previous stitch on the first side (C). Work the next stitch at the same angle, exiting on the opposite side (D).

4. Repeat Step 3 until the shape is filled (E, F, G, H, and I).

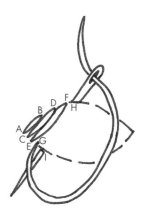

Detail of Daydream (page 134)

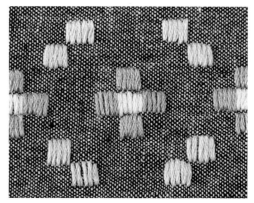

Detail of Pixel (page 135)

HERRINGBONE STITCH

Herringbone Stitch has a lovely open appearance. It is usually worked over straight lines but can also be worked along a curve. It has a lot of potential for variation—see Couching Combinations (page 32), Double Stitches (page 33), and Multicolor Stitches (page 33).

1. Bring the needle out to the front of the fabric (A).

2. Make a long diagonal stitch upward and to the right (B).

3. Bring the needle back out, about ¼˝ to the left-hand side (C). Make a long diagonal stitch downward and to the right (D). Bring the needle back out about ¼˝ to the left (E).

4. Repeat Steps 2 and 3 for the required length (F, G, and H).

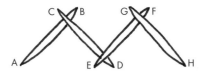

Detail of Primrose (page 123)

FRENCH KNOT

French Knot is a versatile stitch with a pretty, raised bobble-like appearance. It works well in contrast with many other stitches and can be utilized as a flower center: either a single knot on its own or several to fill a central area. French Knot can also be stitched along a straight or curved pattern line.

1. Bring the needle out to the front of the fabric. Reenter and exit the fabric about ⅛˝ apart, with the front half of the needle only.

2. Wrap the thread tightly around the front of the needle 3 times.

3. Hold down the wrapped threads with the thumb of your non-sewing hand. Grab the needle front with the thumb and forefinger of your opposite hand, and gently pull the needle through the wrapped thread.

4. Once the needle has exited the wraps, gently grip them with the thumb and forefinger of your non-sewing hand and push them down toward the fabric. This should make a neat knot close to the fabric surface.

5. Insert the needle behind the knot, and pull the remaining thread out to the back of the fabric.

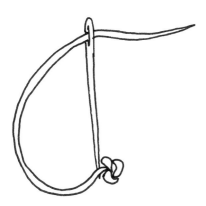

6. Repeat Steps 1–5 to make additional French Knots, or tie off the thread at the back of the fabric.

Detail of Marguerite (page 107)

CHAIN STITCH

Chain Stitch is useful for working straight and curved lines or for outlining elements. It is very decorative in appearance and is composed of a chain made up of linked loops.

1. Bring the needle out to the front of the fabric (A).

2. Make a small loop on the fabric surface, and hold it in place with the thumb of your non-sewing hand. Exit the needle at the same entry point (B), leaving the thread loop loosely in place.

3. Bring the needle back out about ¼˝ along and inside the loop. Pull the needle and thread gently to secure the loop in place (C).

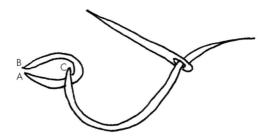

4. Repeat Steps 2 and 3 to work the required length (D and E).

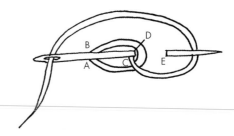

5. To finish a line of stitching, make a small stitch to anchor the final loop in place.

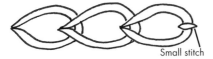

Small stitch

To finish a circular element where the starting point is the same as the end point, wrap the thread around the start of the first loop. Exit the fabric at the entry point of the final loop.

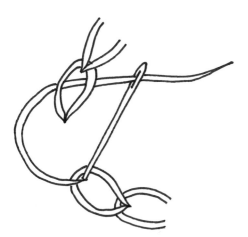

Wrapping the thread around the first loop

Detail of Vignette (page 130)

LAZY DAISY

Lazy Daisy is worked as a single loop anchored to the fabric surface with a small stitch. It can be used to suggest both flower petals and leaves. The stitch length can vary between ¼″–½″ to suit the pattern element. See also Multicolor Stitches (page 33).

1. Bring the needle out to the front of the fabric (A). Make a small loop with the thread on the fabric surface and exit (B).

2. Bring the needle back out about 1 stitch length along and inside the loop (C). Pull the needle and thread gently and exit (D), making a small stitch to anchor the loop in place.

3. Repeat Steps 1 and 2 to make as many Lazy Daisy stitches as required.

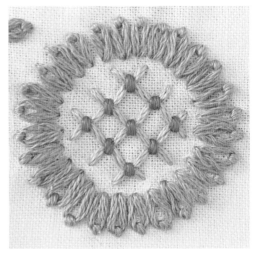

Detail of In Bloom (page 73)

SPLIT STITCH

Split Stitch is worked similarly to Backstitch (page 19), with the exception that the needle is inserted just inside the previous stitch; this splits each stitch as you work. It has a similar look to Chain Stitch (page 23), but the stitches are tighter in appearance.

1. Bring the needle out to the front of the fabric (A). Take a stitch about ¼˝ in length (B).

2. Bring the needle back out to the front of the fabric, about ¼˝ away from where the previous stitch ended (C).

3. Reinsert the needle just inside the previous stitch, splitting the strands of thread evenly (D).

4. Repeat Steps 2 and 3 for the length of the pattern line (E and F).

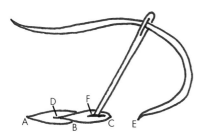

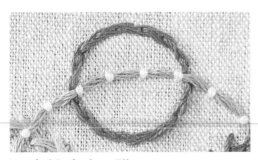

Detail of Circles (page 72)

COUCHING STITCH

This stitch is made using two threads—a laid thread and a couching thread. The laid thread is placed across the fabric along a pattern line. The couching thread is used to stitch over the laid thread at intervals to hold it in place. Usually two contrasting colors are used to give a bold effect.

The laid stitch can be worked as a single long Straight Stitch or several smaller stitches (such as a grid). But for a decorative effect, you can start with a laid thread in a Cross-Stitch or Herringbone Stitch (see Couching Combinations, page 32).

Couching Stitches can be worked as Straight Stitches, Cross-Stitches, or anything else that works.

To Couch Along a Line

1. Choose 2 threads: 1 laid thread and 1 couching thread.

2. Bring the laid thread out to the front of the fabric (A), and lay it over the pattern line. Exit the fabric at the end of the line (B). Make additional laid stitches if necessary. Remove the needle from the thread, if desired, but don't tie off the thread yet.

3. Bring the couching thread out to the front of the fabric (C). Make small stitches over the laid thread at intervals to secure (D, E, F, G, and H). Continue along the length and/or remaining stitches of the laid thread.

4. Exit the fabric with the couching thread. Pull the laid thread gently if needed to lie neatly. Tie off both threads to secure.

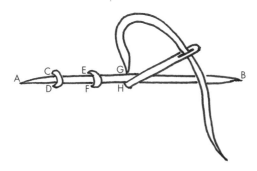

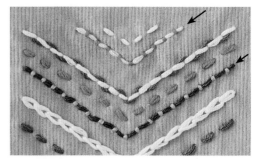

Detail of Herringbone (page 108)

To Couch a Grid

1. Choose 2 threads: 1 laid thread and 1 couching thread.

2. Bring the laid thread out to the front of the fabric (A), and lay it over the first pattern line. Exit the fabric at the end of the line (B). Make the remaining laid stitches in the same way (C, D, E, F, G, H, I, J, K, and L). Remove the needle from the thread, if desired, but don't tie off the thread yet.

3. Bring the couching thread out to the front of the fabric (M). Make small stitches over the laid thread at the intersections to secure

(N, O, P, Q, and R). Continue until all the intersections have been couched.

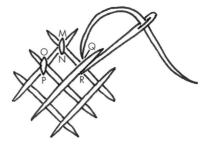

4. Exit the fabric with the couching thread. Pull the laid thread gently if needed to lie neatly. Tie off both threads to secure.

Detail of Fair Isle (page 75)

BLANKET STITCH

This simple stitch works nicely for edging a design.

1. *Optional:* Bring the needle out to the front of the fabric (A). Make a vertical stitch about ¼˝ in length (B).

Step 1 is optional depending on how you want the start to look. This step starts the stitch with a line. In Traveler (page 121), I started at Step 2, without a line. For Pixel (page 135), I used the optional step to start with a line.

2. Bring the needle out (C).

3. Hold the thread below the stitch line with the thumb of your non-sewing hand.

4. Insert the front half of the needle (D) and bring out the needle tip (E).

5. Position the needle tip above the thread; then pull the needle and thread through. Continue to hold the thread down as you pull the needle taut, ensuring that the start of the new stitch anchors the previous stitch securely in place (E).

6. Repeat Steps 3–5 for the required length (F and G).

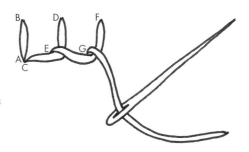

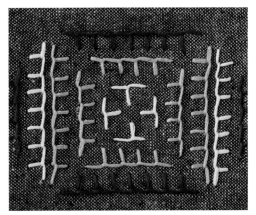

Detail of Traveler (page 121)

FISHBONE STITCH

Fishbone Stitch is useful for working leaves and flower petals. The stitches are worked at an angle, resulting in a glossy appearance.

1. Bring the needle out to the front of the fabric at the top of the shape (A). Make a small vertical stitch about ⅛˝ long (B).

2. Bring the needle out at the top left of the shape (C). Make a diagonal stitch, exiting the fabric to the right-hand side of the centerline (D).

3. Bring the needle back out at the top right of the shape (E). Make a diagonal stitch, exiting the fabric to the left-hand side of the centerline (F).

4. Bring the needle out at the left edge, just below the start of the previous stitch on that side of the shape (G). Make a diagonal stitch, exiting the fabric to the right-hand side of the centerline (H).

5. Bring the needle back out at the right edge, just below the start of the previous stitch on that side of the shape (I). Make a diagonal stitch, exiting the fabric to the left-hand side of the centerline (J).

6. Repeat Steps 4 and 5 until the shape is filled.

Detail of Bouquet (page 120)

VAN DYKE STITCH

This decorative stitch works well for leaf and petal elements in a design. As the stitches are worked, a pretty braid effect forms at the center.

1. Bring the needle and thread out at the left edge of the shape, about ¼˝ from the top (A). Insert the front half of the needle at the top right (B), bringing the tip out at the top left (C). Pull the needle and thread all the way through.

2. Insert the needle at the right edge of the shape, about ¼˝ from the top (D).

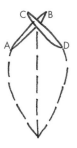

3. Bring the needle out just below the start of the previous stitch on the left edge (E). Insert the needle tip behind the previous set of crossed stitches. (Pass under the threads only—don't exit the fabric.)

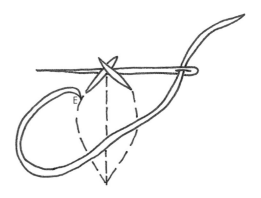

4. Pull the needle and thread through. Insert the needle just below the end of the previous stitch on the right edge (F).

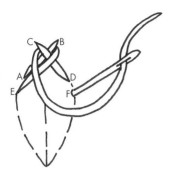

5. Repeat Steps 3 and 4 until the shape is filled.

Detail of Petal (page 106)

SPIDER WEB

This circular stitch starts with laid spokes, around which the thread is wrapped to create a raised textural motif. Spider Web is very useful for stitching decorative flower centers, and it can be worked in one or more colors for different effects. To avoid accidentally snagging the stitch as you work, use a tapestry needle for the weaving element.

1. Make the spokes: Work 4 long Straight Stitches of equal length that cross over a central axis (A, B, C, D, E, F, G, and H).

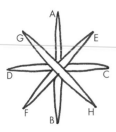

2. Continue with the same thread color, or change to a second contrasting shade. Bring the needle out to the fabric front from behind the center of the spokes (I). Change to a tapestry needle.

3. Wrap the thread over the first spoke. Take the needle under the same spoke and the next spoke (working counterclockwise).

4. Pull tight. Wrap the thread back over the last spoke. Take the needle under the same spoke and the next spoke.

5. Continue working Step 4 all around until the spokes are completely covered. Switch back to an embroidery needle if you wish, and exit behind the web to the back of the work.

Detail of Posy (page 118)

WEAVING STITCH

Usually worked in two thread colors, Weaving Stitch creates a filled area with a basketlike texture. The first thread of the stitch is laid as a set of long Straight Stitches, and the second thread is woven in and out of the laid stitches. To create a stripe or plaid effect, use more than two colors (see Weave, page 89).

1. Bring the needle out to the front of the fabric (A). Make a long stitch to the opposite edge of the shape to be filled (B).

2. Repeat Step 1 to create as many laid stitches as required (C, D, E, F, G, and H). Tie off the first thread color.

3. Using the second thread color, bring the needle out (I). Change to a tapestry needle.

4. Weave the needle and thread in and out of alternate laid stitches.

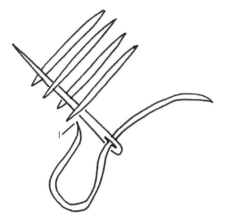

5. Exit the fabric (J). Bring the needle out (K), and weave back across the laid stitches. Start the row by weaving the opposite way to the woven stitch immediately below. If the stitch was woven over the laid stitch, start by weaving behind the first laid stitch, and vice versa.

6. Repeat Step 5 until the laid stitches are woven all the way along (L, M, N, O, and P).

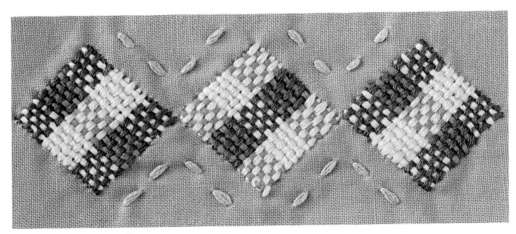

Detail of Weave (page 89)

Embroidery Beyond the Basics

Once you are familiar with the basic stitches, you can use them in a variety of ways to create different results. You can use stitches in combination with each other to create a new stitch or pattern effect, work them in multiple colors, or enhance a basic stitch by lacing through it to create an interesting and dynamic appearance.

STITCH COMBINATIONS

Combine two or more stitches together along the same pattern line to create new effects. The second stitch could be layered onto the first or worked in the gaps between the first set of stitches. Try adding Straight Stitches on top of Cross-Stitches using a different floss color (see the detail of Fair Isle below), or add French Knots in the gaps between a line of Cross-Stitches.

COUCHING COMBINATIONS

Couching Stitch (page 25) is extremely versatile. It can be used in combination with a multitude of other basic stitches to create variations such as Couched Herringbone Stitch or Couched Cross-Stitch. See the detail of Chevron below. In this example, make Herringbone Stitches or Cross-Stitches first as the laid element, and use a second color of floss to couch the stitches.

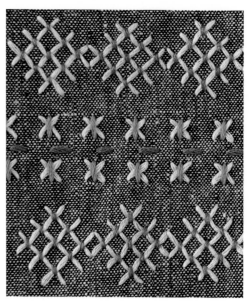

Detail of Fair Isle (page 75)

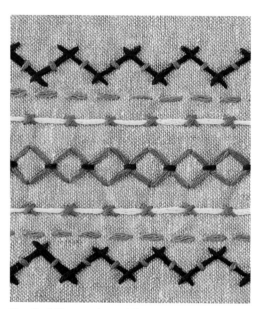

Detail of Chevron (page 90)

DOUBLE STITCHES

You can create interesting effects by simply working the same stitch twice over the same pattern line. Usually a different color of floss is used for each set of stitches. Some stitches that work well as double stitches include double Running Stitch (see the detail of Herringbone below) and double Herringbone Stitch (see the detail of Colorwork below).

To work stitches double, follow these steps:

1. Stitch along the pattern line.

2. Using a different color of floss, embroider a second set of stitches in the gaps left by the first.

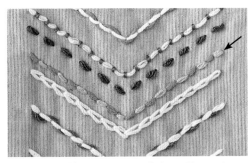

Detail of double Running Stitch from Herringbone (page 108)

Detail of double Herringbone Stitch from Colorwork (page 74)

MULTICOLOR STITCHES

Make a stitch usually worked in one color more unusual by stitching it using two or more shades of thread. Cross-Stitch, Lazy Daisy, and Herringbone Stitch all work really well in this way.

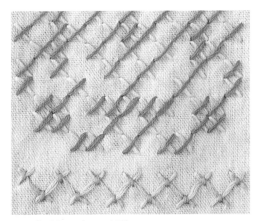

Detail of June (page 105)

Detail of Floret (page 88)

LACING

Make a line of stitches; lace in and out of them using a second color of thread. Pass the lacing thread behind the stitches only. The lacing thread is inserted through the fabric only at the start and end of the stitched line.

Laced Running Stitch

A single line of Running Stitches can be laced, but a far more interesting effect is created by lacing up and down through two lines of stitches.

1. Make 2 lines of Running Stitches (page 18) with small stitches and large gaps (A, B, C, D, E, F, G, H, I, J, K, and L).

2. Bring a second color of thread to the fabric front, and lace up and down through the 2 lines of stitches.

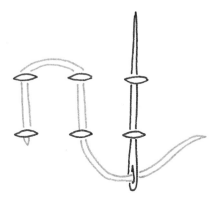

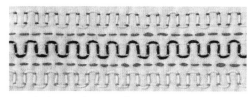

Detail of Curve (page 132)

Laced Backstitch

1. Make a line of Backstitches (page 19).

2. Bring a second color of thread to the fabric front from under the first Backstitch. Lace under the first stitch from the bottom to the top.

3. Lace under the next stitch from the top to the bottom.

4. Lace under the next stitch from the bottom to the top.

5. Repeat Steps 3 and 4 until the end of the stitch line.

6. Take the lacing thread to the back of the fabric under the end of the last Backstitch, and tie off.

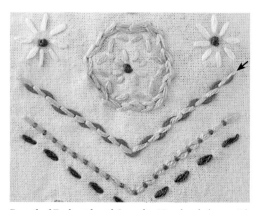

Detail of Embroidered Sampler Notebook (page 45)

Twice-Laced Backstitch

1. Follow Laced Backstitch, Steps 1–5 (previous page).

2. Take the lacing thread to the back of the fabric under the last Backstitch. Reenter the fabric about ⅛″ from the exit point under the last Backstitch.

3. Lace the thread back through, working the thread through the opposite way of the previous lacing stitches.

Start.

Detail of Circles (page 72)

Notebook Embroidery Details

The Embroidered Sampler Notebook (page 62) is a fun exercise to both practice stitches and explore ideas while finding your personal embroidery style. When I was forming my plans for this book, this is how I processed my ideas and developed them into potential patterns.

I'm going to detail how I created the designs in my notebook. I hope this will inspire you to make your own Embroidered Sampler Notebook following the project instructions (page 62). Any time you need a dose of inspiration, flip through the pages and revisit your ideas to kick-start your creativity. Think of it as "thread play," a sketchbook made up of stitches. Try out the possibilities, and think "What if…?"

In keeping with creating a personalized notebook of your own stitch samples, I have provided patterns for only portions of the book pages. You can use these as a starting point to explore from or ignore them entirely. It's up to you.

Project Notes: I stitched the cover using Aurifloss in bright orange, light orange, medium pink, green, gold green, gold yellow, and yellow. I stitched the pages using COSMO floss by LECIEN Co. and Aurifil 12-weight wool thread. Patterns are included after certain pages, but these are only for the motifs that cannot be found elsewhere. For instructions on how to create the stitches, see Embroidery Stitches (page 18) and Embroidery Beyond the Basics (page 32). For sewing instructions, see Embroidered Sampler Notebook (page 62).

COVER

1. Cross-Stitch (multicolor stitches), French Knot

2. Straight Stitch, French Knot

3. Chain Stitch, Lazy Daisy (multicolor stitches), French Knot

4. Laced Backstitch

5. Chain Stitch

6. Running Stitch

Cover detail of Embroidered
Sampler Notebook (page 62)

PAGE ONE

1. Cross-Stitch, Straight Stitch: Work every other Cross-Stitch in a second color of floss, and top them with Straight Stitches using 12-weight wool thread.

2. Running Stitch, Lazy Daisy, French Knot

3. Cross-Stitch (multicolor stitches)

4. Couched grid: Work the laid element in 2 colors of 12-weight wool thread. Couch only the center intersections.

5. Lazy Daisy, French Knot

6. Straight Stitch: Use 4 overlapping stitches, each worked in a different color.

Detail of Embroidered Sampler Notebook (page 62): Page one

PAGES TWO AND THREE

1. Twice-laced Lazy Daisy: Make a row of Lazy Daisy stitches with gaps in between. Lace as described in Twice-Laced Backstitch (page 35).

2. Laced Backstitch

3. Double Running Stitch: Make 2 sets of Running Stitches, each worked in a different floss color, over the same pattern line. The second color is worked in the gaps of the first.

4. Blanket Stitch, Couching Stitch: Make 4 long stitches close together for the laid element. Blanket Stitch is worked as the couching element.

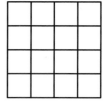

5. Couched Herringbone Stitch: Herringbone Stitch is worked as the laid stitch element.

6. Twice-laced Backstitch

7. Laced Chain Stitch: Make a row of Chain Stitches. Lace as described in Laced Backstitch (page 34).

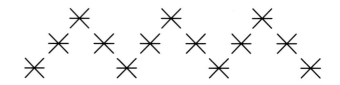

8. Couching Stitch, Cross-Stitch: Work 1 long stitch as the laid element. Cross-Stitch is worked as the couching element.

9. Chain Stitch, Backstitch: Make a row of Chain Stitches. Work Backstitches over the same pattern line, starting each stitch inside a loop and ending in the loop of the following stitch.

10. Backstitch: Work 2 rows, one on top of the other, offset by half a stitch.

11. Laced Running Stitch

12. Spider Web: Use one color of floss for the spokes and a second color for the wrapped element.

13. Spider Web: Use one color for the spokes and the same color for the first 2 rounds of the wrapped element. Use a second color for the next 3 rounds. The first color is used for the final 2 rounds.

14. Spider Web: Use one color for the spokes. Use a second color for 1 round only of the wrapped element.

15. Straight Stitch: Use 4 overlapping stitches, 2 worked in one color and 2 in another.

16. Couched grid

17. Straight Stitch: Make 4 overlapping stitches.

18. Cross-Stitch, Straight Stitch: Top Cross-Stitches (made using 12-weight wool thread) with Straight Stitches in a second color.

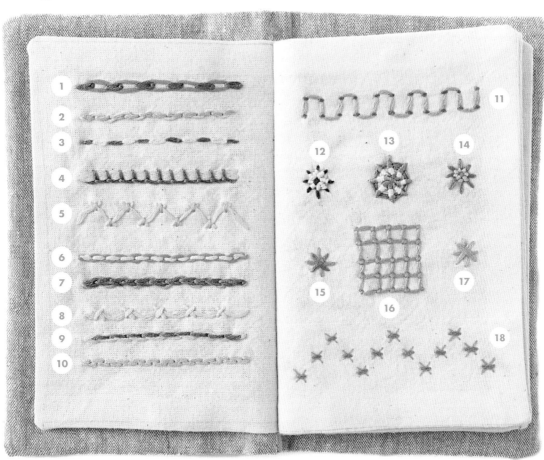

Detail of Embroidered Sampler Notebook (page 62): Pages two and three

PAGES FOUR AND FIVE

1. Couching Stitch: Work along a curved pattern line. Use the same color of floss for both the laid and couching elements.

2. Cross-Stitch, Straight Stitch: Work every other Cross-Stitch in a second color of floss and top them with Straight Stitches in a third color.

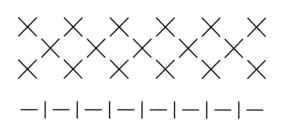

3. Cross-Stitch: Work 3 stitches in color 1, 1 stitch in color 2, 1 stitch in color 3, and 1 stitch in color 2. Repeat the pattern.

4. Cross-Stitch

5. Herringbone Stitch (multicolor stitches)

6. Herringbone Stitch

7. Straight Stitch

8. Lazy Daisy, French Knot

9. Backstitch, Straight Stitch, French Knot: Outline the outer petals in Backstitches, and fill each petal with 5 converging Straight Stitches. Outline the center in Backstitches, with a small grouping of French Knots in the middle.

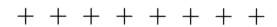

10. Double Running Stitch, Straight Stitch, French Knot: Work Running Stitches in 2 colors of floss over the same pattern line. Work the second color in the gaps of the first.

11. Running Stitch, French Knot

12. Chain Stitch, Cross-Stitch

13. Cross-Stitch: Work vertically instead of diagonally.

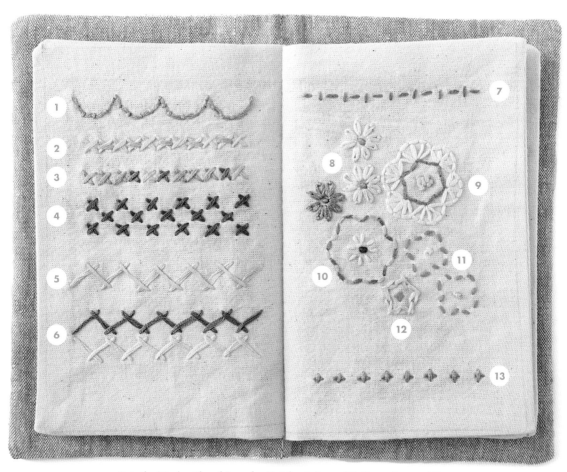

Detail of Embroidered Sampler Notebook (page 62): Pages four and five

PAGES SIX AND SEVEN

1. Cross-Stitch: Work in 12-weight wool thread.

2. Couching Stitch, Cross-Stitch: Work 1 long stitch as the laid element. Work Cross-Stitches as the couching element.

3. Couched Cross-Stitch: Work Cross-Stitches as the laid element.

4. Couched Cross-Stitch: Work horizontal rows of 4 Cross-Stitches. Couch every other Cross-Stitch using 1 of 2 alternating floss colors.

5. Backstitch, Straight Stitch: Outline in Backstitches. Fill each curved element with 7 converging Straight Stitches worked in 12-weight wool thread.

6. Chain Stitch, French Knot

7. Backstitch, Straight Stitch: Work the center stem in Backstitches. Work the leaves in Straight Stitches.

8. Lazy Daisy, French Knot

9. Split Stitch, Straight Stitch: Work the center stem in Split Stitches. Work the leaves in Straight Stitches.

10. Chain Stitch: Work in 12-weight wool thread.

11. Backstitch, Straight Stitch: Outline in Backstitches. Fill each curved element with 7 converging Straight Stitches.

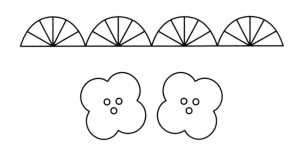

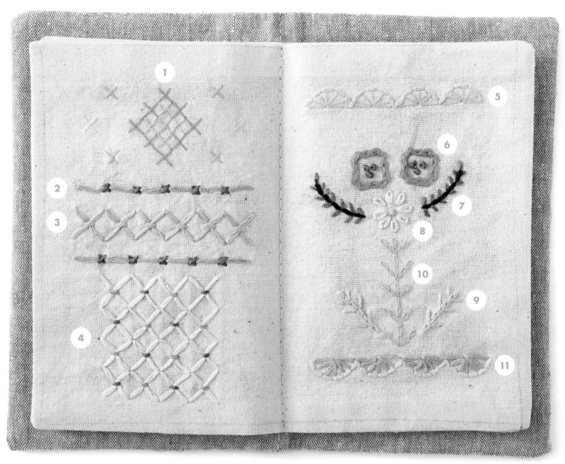

Detail of Embroidered Sampler Notebook (page 62): Pages six and seven

PAGES EIGHT AND NINE

1. Running Stitch, Lazy Daisy, Straight Stitch, French Knot

2. Straight Stitch, French Knot

3. Chain Stitch, Running Stitch, Straight Stitch, French Knot

4. Laced Backstitch

5. Couching Stitch

6. Running Stitch

7. Satin Stitch: Work in 12-weight wool thread.

8. Herringbone Stitch

9. Fishbone Stitch

10. Van Dyke Stitch

11. Fern Stitch

12. Cross-Stitch

13. Straight Stitch, French Knot

14. Cross-Stitch, Straight Stitch, Running Stitch: Overlap each Cross-Stitch with a Straight Stitch worked in the same color floss.

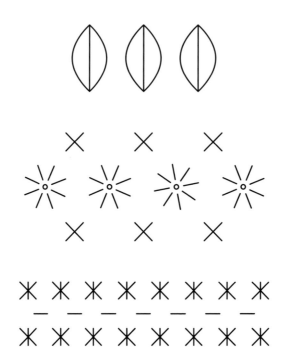

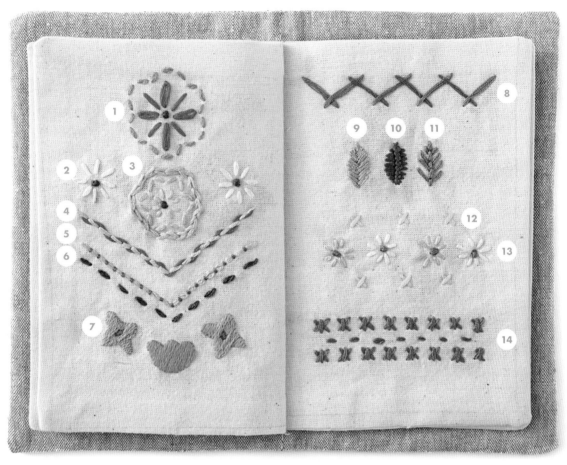

Detail of Embroidered Sampler Notebook (page 62): Pages eight and nine

PAGES TEN, ELEVEN, AND TWELVE

1. Cross-Stitch (multicolor stitches)

2. Backstitch, Straight Stitch

3. Split Stitch, Herringbone Stitch, Couching Stitch: Work Split Stitches in an arrowhead formation. Overlap with a single Couched Herringbone Stitch.

4. Cross-Stitch

5. Weaving Stitch: Work the laid element diagonally from the lower left to the upper right in stripes of 2 colors, with 6 stitches forming each stripe. Work the woven element from the lower right to the upper left in 1 color of floss.

6. Double Herringbone Stitch: Make 2 overlapping rows, each in a different color.

7. Fishbone Stitch

8. Backstitch, Straight Stitch, French Knot

9. Fern Stitch

10. Satin Stitch, French Knot

11. Backstitch, Satin Stitch, Cross-Stitch

12. Cross-Stitch: Work all except one as multicolor stitches in 2 colors.

13. Running Stitch, Straight Stitch

14. Cross-Stitch

15. Blanket Stitch: Work along a curved outline.

16. Fern Stitch

17. Backstitch, Straight Stitch

18. Running Stitch

19. Running Stitch

Detail of Embroidered Sampler Notebook (page 62): Pages ten and eleven

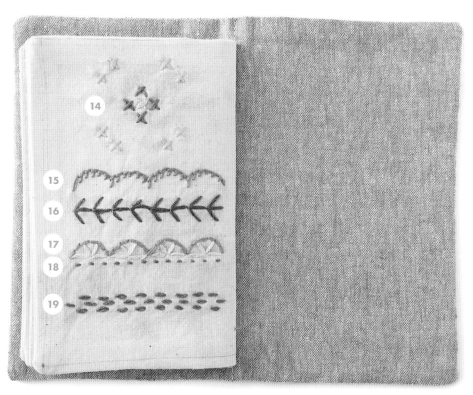

Detail of Embroidered Sampler Notebook (page 62): Page twelve

Embroidery Basics

Sewing Basics

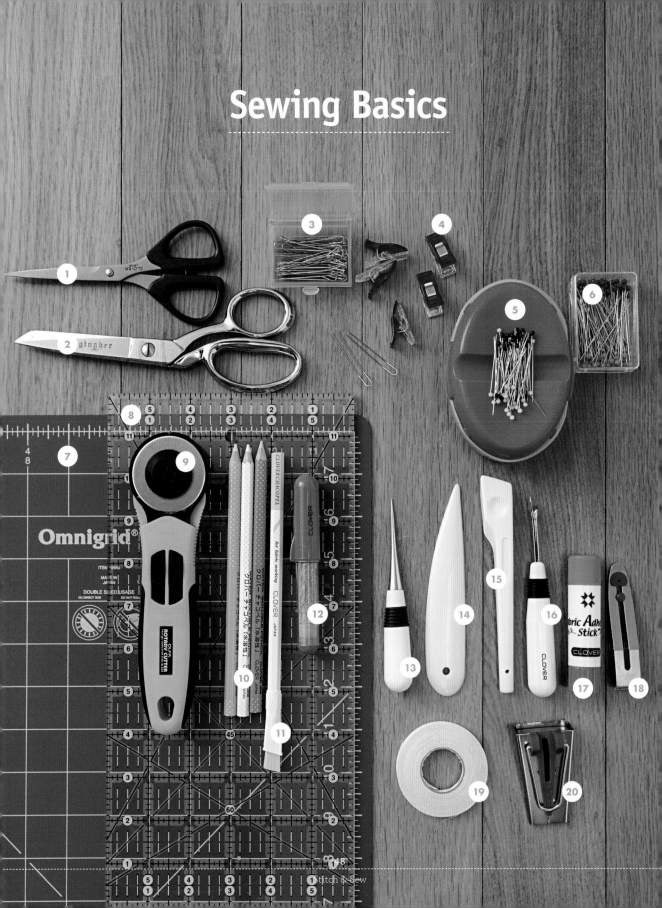

Tools and Equipment

1. Small fabric scissors
2. Gingher fabric scissors
3. Fork pins
4. Binding clips
5. Magnetic pin caddy
6. Glass-head pins
7. Cutting mat

8. Ruler
9. Rotary cutter
10. Water-soluble pencils
11. Clover Chacopel
12. Clover Pen-Style Chaco Liner
13. Awl
14. Point turner

15. Finger presser
16. Seam ripper
17. Fabric glue stick
18. Bodkin
19. Fusible tape
20. Bias tape maker

CUTTING MAT, RULER, AND ROTARY CUTTER ⑦–⑨

These tools are essential for accurately cutting fabric. The cutting mat and ruler will also be helpful when positioning the patterns.

SCISSORS ① and ②

Use fabric scissors when cutting curved edges or cutting out darts or squares for boxed seams. Keep a separate pair of scissors for cutting paper and other materials.

MARKING TOOLS FOR SEWING ⑩–⑫

There are a variety of marking tools available for sewing, but I mostly use Chaco Liners by Clover (a chalk liner in pen form) and water-soluble pencils. It can be useful to have several colors on hand for marking different fabric colors.

It is worth emphasizing here that I use embroidery marking pens (page 12) during the embroidery part of the project only—up to the point of washing out the embroidery pattern (see Removing Embroidery Marking-Pen Lines, page 17).

I use Chaco Liners or water-soluble pencils for the sewing part of the project and mark only within the seam allowance. This avoids having marks left in visible areas of the finished project.

PINS ⑥

Use pins to secure the fabric temporarily before sewing. I like glass-head pins the best. I would also recommend using a magnetic pin caddy ⑤, which allows you to quickly drop pins onto it as you sew. It really speeds things up!

FORK PINS ③

These U-shaped pronged pins have two sharp points. Use them when sewing crossing seams (see Aligning Crossing Seams, page 58).

BINDING CLIPS ④

I find these indispensable for holding bulky fabric layers together securely.

FUSIBLE TAPE ⑲

This heat-activated tape is useful for quickly fusing batting to fabric in projects (see Using Fusible Tape, page 55).

FABRIC GLUE STICK ⑰

A fabric glue stick temporarily adheres surfaces together wherever pins would be tricky to use, such as when sewing zipper end tabs (page 55). The stick format makes for easy use and less mess than other fabric glues.

FINGER PRESSER ⑮

This simple tool is handy for creasing fabric when placing the patterns (see Positioning the Pattern, page 13). It can also be used to temporarily press seam allowances open or turn fabric edges while sewing prior to pressing with an iron. To use, fold fabric where needed and run the finger presser along the fold.

POINT TURNER ⑭

Use this tool when turning projects right side out after sewing. Insert the point turner into the wrong side of the sewn item, and *gently* push along the seams and into the corners to turn them out neatly.

BIAS TAPE MAKER ⑳

These time-saving gadgets can be used to fold fabric strips quickly for making fabric ties. They are sized by the width of the prepared strip when it comes out of the tape maker. The finished width of the fabric tie will be half of this. Use the 1″ size to make ½″ ties for the Drawstring Pouch (page 68).

BODKIN ⑱

Use a bodkin to insert fabric ties into a finished project (see Drawstring Pouch, page 68).

AWL ⑬

I find it good practice to hold an awl in my hand as I sew. I use the awl to smooth the fabric down as it reaches the presser foot and help guide the fabric through as needed. It is especially handy when sewing zippers or bulky seams and means that I'm not tempted to use my fingers to help navigate the fabric near the presser foot (see the tip in Aligning Zipper Seams, page 57).

SEAM RIPPER ⑯

Seam rippers easily remove stitches when things go wrong.

Materials

1. Yarn-dyed metallic linen
2. Quilting cotton
3. Canvas
4. Flannel
5. Fine-ribbed corduroy or needlecord
6. Lawn
7. Yarn-dyed linen
8. Aurifil thread
9. Flex frame and pin
10. Metal zipper
11. Fusible fleece
12. Woven interfacing
13. Batting
14. Leather

FABRIC ①–⑦

The sewing projects in this book will require additional fabrics for linings, channels, ties, and other details. When selecting fabrics, choose carefully to complement the exterior fabric. Combining different fabric types together in a project works well to enhance the tactile element of a finished item with textural contrast. Fabric types to consider include yarn-dyed linen (or yarn-dyed metallic linen), needlecord (a finely ribbed corduroy), lawn, quilting cotton, canvas, chambray, and flannel.

THREAD ⑧

Use a good quality 100% cotton thread for best results. I use a multipurpose Aurifil 50-weight thread and the thicker 28-weight thread for all my sewing projects. The 28-weight thread has a beautiful finish when used for topstitching, as it allows the stitches to stand out a little more. My most-used thread color is a pale pink, which works nicely with many different fabric colors. Think of it as a pretty neutral.

INTERFACING ⑪–⑬

The projects are interfaced with woven fusible interfacing, fusible fleece, or batting. These will provide structure and body to the sewn item.

- I use either Pellon SF101 Shape-Flex (20″ wide) or Vilene G 700 (35″ wide) for woven interfacing. *Note the different widths*—interfacing yardage requirements in this book are all based on 20″ width.

- I use a low-loft fusible fleece, either Pellon 987F (45″ wide) or Vilene H 630 (35″ wide). Fusible fleece yardage requirements in this book are based on 45″ width. Use a pressing cloth when pressing fusible fleece to prevent it from sticking to your iron.

- For batting, I use Quilters Dream Cotton in Request or Select weight. (Scraps left over from quilt projects will work nicely.)

ZIPPERS ⑩

Zippers with either metal or nylon teeth will work well for the projects in this book. I find Zipit on Etsy (etsy.com) to be a great resource for both types. I used metal zippers throughout this book, as I feel they give a stylish finish. My favorite zippers are those with gold metal teeth and donut-shaped pulls.

FLEX FRAME ⑨

A flex frame has two flexible metal sides with a closed hinge at one end and an open hinge at the other. The open hinge is secured once the frame has been inserted into the sewn item, such as the Flex Case (page 102). Once inserted, squeeze the short ends of the frame to pop open the case.

LEATHER ⑭

You can use leather strips as ties or zipper pulls for the projects. You will need strips or scrap pieces, which you can find online through many producers of leather goods. Leather with a thickness of about $\frac{1}{16}''$ will work well. For the ties of the Drawstring Pouch (page 68), I used flat leather strips with a width of $\frac{1}{8}''$, but anywhere between $\frac{1}{8}''-\frac{1}{4}''$ would work equally well. For the zipper-pull details of the Clutch (page 86), Small Change Purse (page 116), and Zipper Pouch (page 128), I used scrap leather pieces and cut them about $\frac{3}{16}''$ wide. You can cut the leather using a rotary cutter, but don't use the same blade that you use for cutting fabric. An older blade that is too dull for fabric will cut the leather fine.

Sewing Techniques

SEWING MACHINE SETTINGS

There are several settings that I constantly use when sewing projects like pouches and cases. To enable these on your machine, check the manual. You should be able to access this online if you don't have it on hand.

Backstitch

Use this setting at the start and end of all seams to secure them. You can also do this manually by making a few stitches, reversing, and stitching over them a second time.

Needle Down

Using this setting will ensure that every time you stop mid-seam, the needle will remain in the down position. This stops accidental movement and will enable neat pivoting at corners.

Stitch Length

Use a longer stitch length when topstitching, sewing through multiple layers, or machine basting. Use a shorter stitch length when sewing curves for a neater finish.

Sewing Machine Free Arm

Removing the extension table from your machine will expose the free arm. This will enable you to rotate projects around it as you sew.

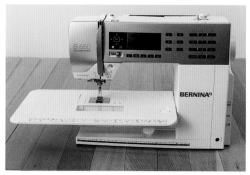

Sewing machine with extension table attached

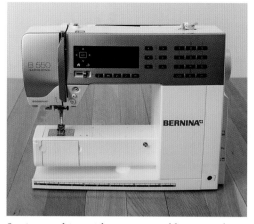

Sewing machine with extension table removed

PRESSING

Press using an iron whenever indicated. You can pre-open the seams by temporarily creasing with a finger presser (page 50) prior to pressing with an iron.

USING FUSIBLE TAPE

Use fusible tape to quickly and easily fuse batting to fabric.

1. Cut strips of the required length.

2. Place the strips, rough side down, along the edges of the batting. Press to fuse the strips to the batting. Allow to cool.

3. Peel off the paper backing from the tape. Position the batting, tape side down, onto the wrong side of the fabric. Press to fuse the batting to the fabric.

ZIPPER BASICS

Zippers are sized by the measurement between the top of the zipper pull and the bottom stop. The total length of the zipper tape will be about 1½″ longer (¾″ at each short end) than the zipper measurement. Use a zipper foot when sewing zippers, and adjust the needle position if necessary to get the required ¼″ seam allowance. The right side of the zipper is the side with the zipper teeth and pull.

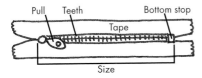

Trimming Zippers

Before you install a zipper, trim the excess tape at each short end to ⅜″. Measure ⅜″ from the pull, mark a line across the zipper tape, and cut along the line. Repeat to cut ⅜″ away from the bottom stop. The finished length of the zipper tape will be ¾″ longer than the zipper measurement.

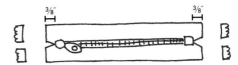

Sewing Zipper End Tabs

1. Fold each 1½″ × 1″ zipper tab rectangle in half, wrong sides together, so the folded tab measures ¾″ × 1″; press. Unfold. Fold the short edges toward the center crease on the wrong side and press.

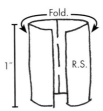

Fold short ends to center crease.

2. Bring the folded edges together so each tab measures ⅜″ × 1″. Press.

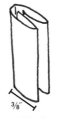

Fold tab in half.

3. Unfold at the center. Using a fabric glue stick, dab a little glue onto the folded edges of each tab. Leave to dry for 30 seconds.

Glue on the folded edges

4. Slip the tabs over the short ends of the trimmed zipper, and leave to dry for 10 minutes. Topstitch ⅛″ from the fold to attach.

Sew tabs to zipper.

Sewing Zippers

Install your zipper using a zipper foot and a ¼″ seam allowance. I use the needle-down setting (page 54) so that I can stop mid-seam, raise the presser foot, and move the zipper pull out of the way before continuing the seam.

1. Place 1 lining rectangle right side up. Center the zipper with the right side facing up along the top edge of the lining. The closed zipper pull should be at the right-hand side.

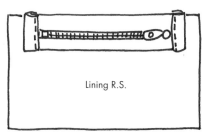

Lining R.S.

Zipper centered on lining's right side

2. Place 1 exterior rectangle, wrong side up, on top. Align the top and side edges of the fabric; pin. Sew with a zipper foot, using a ¼″ seam allowance.

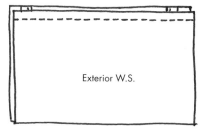

Exterior W.S.

Exterior layered on top, wrong side up. Sew.

3. Refold so the assembled piece is wrong sides together, with the edges aligned.

4. Place the second lining rectangle right side up. Place the assembled piece on top, with the exterior facing up and the zipper aligned at the top edge. The open zipper pull should be at the right-hand side.

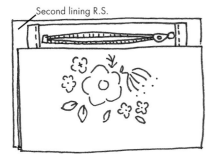

Second lining right side up with assembled piece on top, zipper open

5. Place the second exterior rectangle, wrong side up, on top. Align the top and side edges. Pin and sew using a ¼″ seam allowance.

6. Refold so the assembled piece is wrong sides together with the edges aligned. Press. Topstitch along both sides of the zipper.

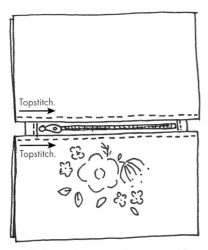

One lining and one exterior wrong sides together on either side of zipper

ALIGNING SEAMS

Here are a couple of tips I use to help align zipper seams and crossing seams in projects.

Aligning Zipper Seams

1. Before sewing the exterior and lining pieces right sides together, push the zipper and tabs (sandwiched between the fabrics) toward the lining. The zipper will fold neatly in half lengthwise and push the zipper seam allowance toward the exterior. This will make it easier to align the zipper seams at the side edges and ensure a neat finish.

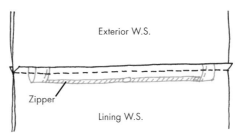

Folded zipper viewed between fabrics

2. Pin at each end of the zipper seam to secure. Continue according to the project directions. When sewing the side edges, make sure to sew *alongside* the tabs and not through them.

TIP

When you reach the center part of the side seams, the bulky zipper tabs may lift your presser foot unevenly, leading to skipped stitches. Insert the tip of an awl (page 50) under the other half of the presser foot to help balance it and make it easier to sew smoothly.

Aligning Crossing Seams

1. Press the seam allowances open.

2. Align the seams at the center, and pin in place with a fork pin. Insert half of the pin into each side of the seam allowance.

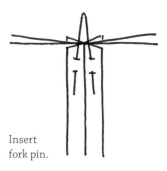

Insert
fork pin.

3. Sew along the seam.

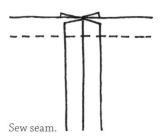

Sew seam.

TURNING RIGHT SIDES OUT

After a project has been sewn right sides together, follow these steps:

1. Press the seams open, including at the gap that you have left for turning right side out.

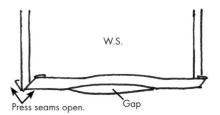

W.S.

Press seams open.   Gap

2. Make the corners less bulky by trimming square corners and clipping curves.

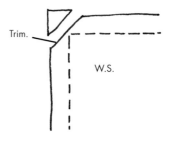

Trim.

W.S.

Trim square corner.

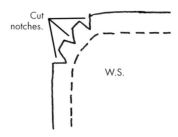

Cut
notches.

W.S.

Clip curved corner.

3. Turn right side out. Use a point turner (page 50) to push out corners neatly. Press.

SEWING THE GAP CLOSED

After the sewn item has been turned right side out, sew the gap closed either by hand or machine depending on personal preference. Use a thread color to match the fabric.

By Hand

This method yields a neater end result.

1. Pin the 2 sides of fabric to be joined together. Make a few Backstitches within the seam allowance to secure the thread end. Bring the needle and thread out through one of the folded fabric edges.

2. Make a horizontal stitch across to the opposite folded edge. Bring the needle out about ¼″ along the folded edge.

3. Repeat Step 2 until the gap has been sewn closed. Secure the thread end and cut the excess.

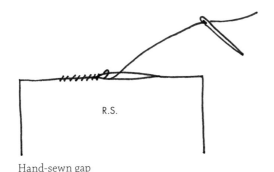

R.S.

Hand-sewn gap

By Machine

This method is quicker but will be more noticeable in the finished item.

1. Pin the 2 sides of the gap together.

2. Machine sew along the gap, close to the folded edge. Backstitch at the start and end of the seam.

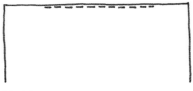

Machine-sewn gap

Project Notes

- Dimensions are written as width × height throughout.

- Backstitch at the start and end of all seams.

- Use a longer stitch for topstitching.

- *Lengthwise* means parallel to the length.

- *Widthwise* means parallel to the width.

- A standard fat quarter is 18″ × 21″.

- A standard fat eighth is 9″ × 21″.

- In the illustrations throughout this book, *R.S.* represents the right side of the fabric and *W.S.* represents the wrong side of the fabric.

- Aurifloss by Aurifil was used to embroider all projects, except where noted.

Projects

Finished notebook: 4½″ wide × 7″ high × 1″ deep

Embroidered Sampler Notebook

Create an embroidery sampler in book form to learn and practice stitches, explore ideas, and inspire your projects!

MATERIALS

Cover: 1 fat quarter of chambray, cotton, or yarn-dyed linen

Lining: 1 fat quarter of yarn-dyed linen or cotton

Pages: ⅝ yard of canvas, cotton, or yarn-dyed linen

Batting: 10″ × 10″ square

Embroidery floss

Embroidery hoop: 5″

Fusible tape (⅜″ wide): 1 yard, such as Clover fusible web (#4032)

CUTTING

Cover

• Cut 1 rectangle 12″ × 10″.

Lining

• Cut 1 rectangle 10″ × 8″.

Pages

• Cut 6 rectangles 11″ × 9″.

Batting

• Cut 1 rectangle 9″ × 7″ for the cover.

Style Notes

Cover: Chambray Union in Indigo · Lining: Essex Yarn Dyed linen in Berry · Aurifloss

Pages: Canvas · COSMO floss by LECIEN Co. · Aurifil 12-weight wool thread

Embroidery

INTERIOR PAGES

1. Fold a page rectangle in half lengthwise and crease with a finger presser. Repeat to crease the fabric widthwise.

2. Using the crease marks as a guide, draw an 8″ × 6″ rectangle at the center of the fabric's right side using an embroidery marking pen (page 12). This is the finished size to use as a guide when stitching. Draw a vertical line down the center of the rectangle.

3. Repeat Steps 1 and 2 for all 6 fabric pages.

4. Choose the patterns or design elements using the ideas discussed in Notebook Embroidery Details (page 35) as a guide. Transfer your embroidery choices onto the right side of the fabric (see Transferring Patterns, page 14). Note that each page rectangle is divided into 2 book pages by the drawn centerline. Keep motifs at the center of each individual book page, leaving a clear margin all around.

5. Embroider the pages as you wish.

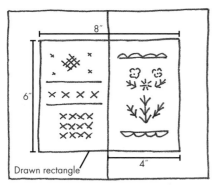

Embroidered rectangle becomes two book pages: a page set.

COVER

1. Repeat Interior Pages, Steps 1 and 2 with the cover, this time drawing a 9″ × 7″ rectangle.

2. Choose the patterns or design elements using the ideas presented in Notebook Embroidery Details (page 35) as a guide. Center the chosen design on the right-hand side of the drawn vertical line and embroider. This is the front cover; the left-hand side of the rectangle is the back cover.

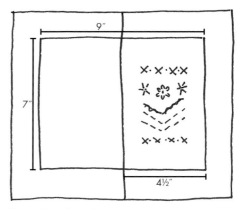

Embroidered notebook cover

Sewing Directions

All seam allowances are ½″ unless otherwise noted.

PREPARATION

Remove the embroidered fabric from the hoop. Wash away any pattern marks or stabilizer; press. See Preparing Embroidered Fabric for Sewing (page 16).

PAGES

1. On each embroidered set of pages, draw a 9″ × 7″ rectangle at the center using a marking tool (page 49). This is the cutting line.

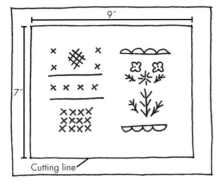

Draw cutting line.

2. Cut along the line.

3. Place 2 page sets right sides together, aligning the edges; pin. Sew around the edge, leaving a 4″ gap at the bottom center. Press the seam open and trim the corners. Turn right side out and press.

4. Repeat with the 4 remaining page sets to create a total of 3 finished page sets, each made up of 4 individual pages front and back.

5. Hand sew the gaps closed (see Sewing the Gap Closed, page 59).

COVER

1. Draw a 10″ × 8″ rectangle at the center of the cover. This is the cutting line.

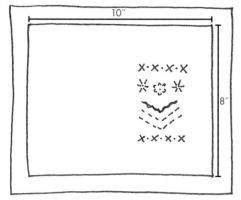

Draw cutting line.

2. Cut out the cover along the drawn line. Cut lengths of fusible tape, and use them to attach the batting to the center of the cover's wrong side (see Using Fusible Tape, page 55).

3. Place the cover and lining fabrics right sides together. Pin and sew around the edge, leaving a 4″ gap at the bottom center. Press the seam open and trim the corners.

4. Turn right side out and press. Hand sew the gap closed (see Sewing the Gap Closed, page 59).

NOTEBOOK ASSEMBLY

1. Place the cover with its lining right side up. Draw a vertical line down the center.

2. Layer the 3 page sets on top of one another at the center of the cover. Use binding clips to secure.

3. Draw a vertical line down the center of the topmost page set, aligned with the line made in Step 1.

4. Using a longer stitch length, sew on the line to attach the pages to the cover.

Sew pages to cover.

Finished pouch: 9″ wide × 9″ high × 4″ deep

Drawstring Pouch

MATERIALS

Exterior: ⅜ yard of yarn-dyed linen, cotton, or canvas

Lining: ⅜ yard of cotton or flannel

Channel: ⅛ yard of cotton, lawn, or fine-ribbed corduroy

Ties: ¼ yard of cotton, lawn, or fine-ribbed corduroy *or* 2 strips of leather ⅛″ × 30″

Embroidery floss

Embroidery hoop: 8″

Bodkin (page 50)

Bias tape maker (page 50): 1″ for ties (*optional*)

CUTTING

Exterior

• Cut 1 square 12″ × 12″ for the front.

• Cut 1 square 10″ × 10″ for the back.

Lining

• Cut 2 squares 10″ × 10″.

Channel

• Cut 2 strips 10″ × 3″.

Ties (*if using fabric*)

• Cut 2 strips 30″ × 2″.

Embroidery

Choose one of the six embroidery options (pages 70–75) to stitch onto the pouch's exterior front. You could also choose to stitch a pattern from another project instead—just make sure it is 8½″ × 5″ or smaller in size.

1. Transfer the chosen design 2½″ down from the top edge and centered across the width. See Positioning the Pattern (page 13) and Transferring Patterns (page 14).

2. Fix the fabric in the hoop. Stitch the embroidery as you wish, or follow the stitch instruction details on the photo.

Drawstring Pouch

BUTTERCUP

Style Notes

Exterior: Essex Yarn Dyed linen in Black • Lining and channel: Quilting cotton • Ties: Leather • Embroidery floss: Orange, gold, blue, yellow, coral, light pink, and light gray

Stitch Guide

See pattern (page 80). See Embroidery Stitches (page 18) for stitch instructions.

1. French Knot

2. Lazy Daisy

3. Cross-Stitch

4. Straight Stitch

5. Backstitch

VINTAGE

Style Notes

Exterior: Canvas • Lining: Quilting cotton • Channel: Cambridge cotton lawn in Gold • Ties: Cambridge cotton lawn in Nude • Embroidery floss: Gold, coral, navy blue, orange, medium pink, light pink, very dark green, green, and white

Stitch Guide

See pattern (page 81). See Embroidery Stitches (page 18) for stitch instructions.

1. Cross-Stitch

CIRCLES

Style Notes

Exterior: Essex Yarn Dyed linen in Oyster · Lining: Quilting cotton · Channel: Essex Yarn Dyed Metallic linen in Dusty Rose · Ties: Corduroy 21 Wale in Pink · Embroidery floss: Red pink, deep pink, medium pink, pink, light pink, and coral

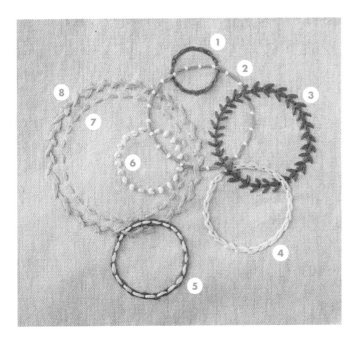

Stitch Guide

See pattern (page 82). See Embroidery Stitches (page 18) for stitch instructions.

1. Split Stitch

2. Couching Stitch

3. Fern Stitch

4. Chain Stitch

5. Twice-laced Backstitch

6. French Knot

7. Running Stitch

8. Herringbone Stitch

STITCH NOTES. See also Twice-Laced Backstitch (page 35).

IN BLOOM

Style Notes

Exterior: Bella Solids in White Bleached · Lining: Quilting cotton · Channel: Cambridge cotton lawn in Nude · Ties: Quilting cotton · Embroidery floss: Gold, yellow-green, light pink, light orange, bright coral, coral, medium pink, and deep gold

Stitch Guide

See pattern (page 83). See Embroidery Stitches (page 18) for stitch instructions.

1. Lazy Daisy

2. Running Stitch

3. Backstitch

4. French Knot

5. Straight Stitch

6. Couched grid

7. Cross-Stitch

8. Split Stitch

9. Spider Web

COLORWORK

Style Notes

Exterior: Essex Yarn Dyed linen in Steel · Lining: Flannel · Channel: Corduroy 21 Wale in Pink · Ties: Leather · Embroidery floss: Dark purple, medium purple, pink, pale pink, orange, brown, gold, pale gray, and white · 12-weight wool thread: Coral and pink

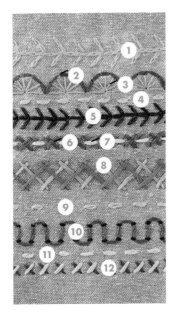

Stitch Guide

See pattern (page 84). See Embroidery Stitches (page 18) for stitch instructions.

1. Chain Stitch (12-weight wool)

2. Backstitch

3. Straight Stitch (12-weight wool)

4. Running Stitch

5. Fern Stitch

6. Cross-Stitch

7. Straight Stitch

8. Double Herringbone Stitch

9. Running Stitch

10. Laced Running Stitch

11. Running Stitch

12. Cross-Stitch (multicolor stitches)

STITCH NOTES. For double Herringbone Stitch, see Double Stitches (page 33); see also Laced Running Stitch (page 34) and Multicolor Stitches (page 33). For the fifth row from the top, use two colors of floss to stitch alternate Cross-Stitches. Top every other Cross-Stitch with a Straight Stitch using a third color of floss.

FAIR ISLE

Stitch Guide

See pattern (page 85). See Embroidery Stitches (page 18) for stitch instructions.

1. Couched grid

2. Cross-Stitch

3. Straight Stitch

4. Running Stitch

STITCH NOTES. For the center row, top each Cross-Stitch with a vertical Straight Stitch using a second color of floss.

Sewing Directions

All seam allowances are ½″ unless otherwise noted.

PREPARATION

1. Remove the embroidered fabric from the hoop. Wash away any pattern marks or stabilizer; press. See Preparing Embroidered Fabric for Sewing (page 16).

2. Trim the front to 10″ × 10″, keeping the embroidery 1½″ from the top edge and centered across the width.

3. Draw and cut out a 2″ square from each bottom corner on both exteriors and both linings.

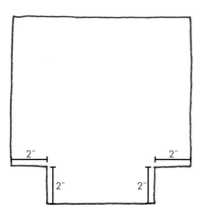

CHANNEL

1. Fold both short edges of 1 channel strip ⅜″ to the wrong side; press. Fold each side in ⅜″ again and press. Repeat with the second channel strip.

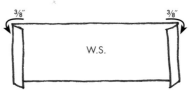

Fold short ends in ⅜″.

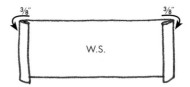

Fold short ends in ⅜″ again.

2. Topstitch ¼″ from the short edges to secure.

3. Fold each of the strips in half widthwise with the wrong sides together; press. The finished width of the channel pieces should be 8½″ or less.

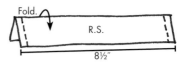

Finished channel strips

TIES

1. Fold each of the short sides on 1 tie fabric strip ½˝ to the wrong side. Press. Fold the strip in half lengthwise, with the wrong sides together, and press.

2. Unfold at the center. Bring the long raw edges toward the crease on the wrong side and press.

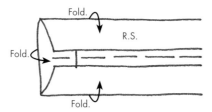

3. Fold in half lengthwise again and press. Sew along the double-folded edge.

4. Repeat Steps 1–3 with the second tie fabric strip.

TIP

Alternatively, use a 1˝ bias tape maker to fold and press the strips. Finish the short ends by unfolding at each end, folding the fabric ½˝ to the wrong side, and refolding the long edges. Fold the strip in half lengthwise and press. Sew along the double-folded edge.

POUCH ASSEMBLY

1. Place the pouch's front right side up. Align the raw edges of a folded channel strip with the top edge of the exterior, centering the channel strip. Pin and machine baste. Repeat with the exterior back and second channel strip.

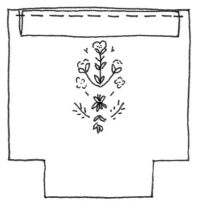

Baste channel to exterior.

2. Pin the exterior front and back pieces with right sides facing. Sew together at the side and bottom edges.

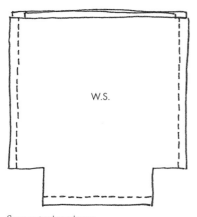

Sew exterior pieces.

3. Press the seams open. At one of the bottom corners, bring the cut-out sides together, aligning the side and bottom seams at the center. Pin and sew to create a boxed corner. Repeat on the opposite corner.

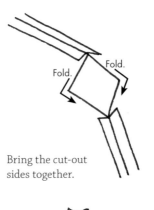

Bring the cut-out sides together.

Sew the boxed corner.

TIP

Use fork pins to align the side and bottom seams perfectly (see Aligning Crossing Seams, page 58).

4. Repeat Steps 2 and 3 with the 2 lining pieces, this time leaving a 4″ gap in the bottom seam.

5. Turn the pouch lining right sides out and insert it into the pouch exterior, right sides facing. Align the top edges and side seams of both pieces. Pin and sew all around the top edge using the sewing machine free arm (page 54).

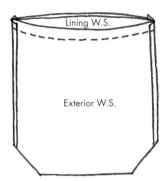

Sew top edge of pouch.

6. Press the seam open. Turn the pouch right side out; press.

7. Topstitch around the top edge of the pouch, just below the channel. Sew the lining gap closed (page 59).

8. Using a bodkin, insert a tie or leather strip through a channel opening. Push all the way around both channel pieces and bring it out on the same side.

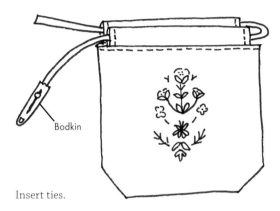

Insert ties.

9. Repeat with the second tie on the opposite side of the channel. Knot the short ends of each tie together.

Patterns

Optional: Download and print Buttercup, Vintage, Circles, In Bloom, Colorwork, or Fair Isle (see Using Patterns, page 13).

Buttercup

Circles

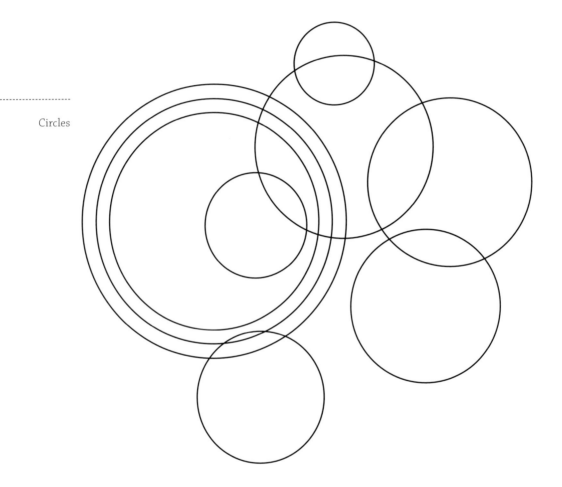

In Bloom

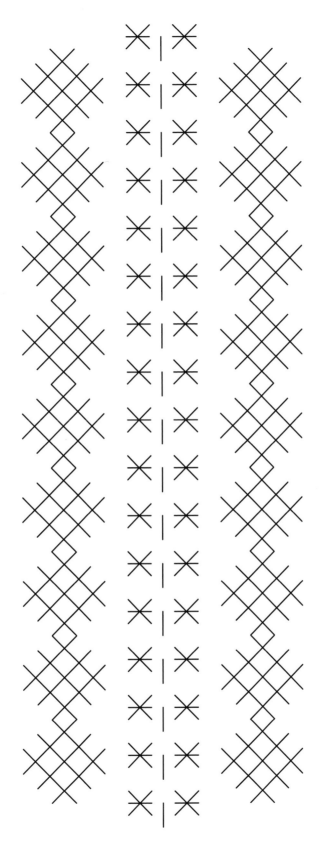

Fair Isle

Finished clutch: 9″ wide × 5″ high × 1¼″ deep

Clutch

MATERIALS

Exterior: ⅜ yard of yarn-dyed linen, quilting cotton, canvas, or chambray

Lining: ¼ yard of yarn-dyed linen, quilting cotton, or yarn-dyed metallic linen

Woven fusible interfacing (20″ wide): ⅜ yard

Fusible fleece (45″ wide): ¼ yard

Zipper: 8″

Fabric glue stick, such as the Clover Fabric Adhesive Stick (#514), for attaching zipper tabs

Zipper pull: ³⁄₁₆″ × 4½″ leather strip (*optional*)

Embroidery floss

Embroidery hoop: 8″

CUTTING

Make a Clutch pattern by joining Clutch pattern pieces A and B (pages 100 and 101). Mark the darts; do not cut them out until instructed.

Exterior

• Cut 1 rectangle 12″ × 10″ for the front.

• Cut 2 rectangles 1½″ × 1″ for the zipper tabs.

• Cut 1 for the back using the Clutch pattern.

Lining

• Cut 2 using the Clutch pattern.

Woven interfacing

• Cut 2 using the Clutch pattern.

Fusible fleece

• Cut 2 using the Clutch pattern's dashed line.

Embroidery

Choose one of the six embroidery options (pages 88–93) to stitch on the clutch's exterior front. You could also choose to stitch a pattern from another project instead—just make sure it is 8½″ × 3″ or smaller in size.

1. Position the clutch's front with the long edges at the top and bottom.

2. Transfer the chosen design 3½″ down from the top edge and centered across the width. See Positioning the Pattern (page 13) and Transferring Patterns (page 14).

3. Fix the fabric in the hoop. Stitch the embroidery as you wish, or follow the stitch instruction details on the photo.

FLORET

Style Notes

Exterior: Chambray · Lining: Quilting cotton · Embroidery floss: Bright orange, light orange, medium green, dark green, khaki, light gray, and white

Stitch Guide

See pattern (page 96). See Embroidery Stitches (page 18) for stitch instructions.

1. Lazy Daisy

2. French Knot

3. Running Stitch

4. Chain Stitch

5. Spider Web

6. Cross-Stitch

7. Backstitch

WEAVE

Style Notes

Exterior: Bella Solids in French Blue • Lining: Essex Yarn Dyed linen in Black • Embroidery floss: Navy blue, orange, pale pink, gray, and light gray

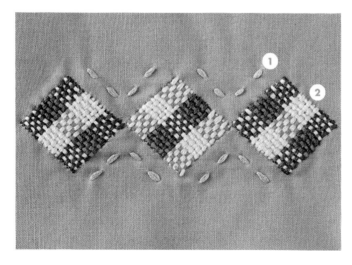

Stitch Guide

See pattern (page 96). See Embroidery Stitches (page 18) for stitch instructions.

1. Running Stitch

2. Weaving Stitch

STITCH NOTES. For Weaving Stitch (page 30), work the colors as follows:

• Central square: Work laid stitches—6 light gray, 6 navy blue, and 6 light gray. Work Weaving Stitches—4 orange, 4 pale pink, and 4 orange.

• Outer squares: Work laid stitches—6 navy blue, 6 light gray, and 6 navy blue. Work Weaving Stitches—4 pale pink, 4 orange, and 4 pale pink.

CHEVRON

Style Notes

Exterior: Essex Yarn Dyed linen in Steel • Lining: Essex Yarn Dyed Metallic linen in Black • Embroidery floss: Dark purple, medium purple, gray, light pink, and orange

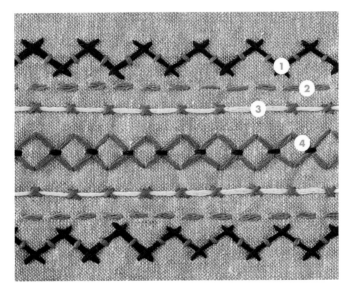

Stitch Guide

See pattern (page 97). See Embroidery Stitches (page 18) for stitch instructions.

1. Couched Herringbone Stitch

2. Running Stitch

3. Couching Stitch

4. Couched Cross-Stitch

STITCH NOTES. For Couched Herringbone Stitch and Couched Cross-Stitch, see Couching Combinations (page 32).

PLAID

Style Notes

Exterior: Canvas • Lining:
Quilting cotton • Embroidery
floss: Gold • 12-weight wool
thread: Yellow and coral

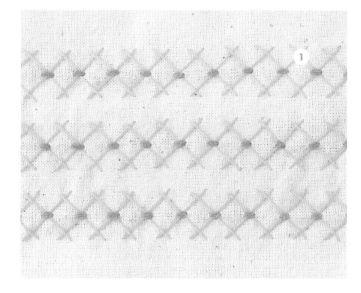

Stitch Guide

See pattern (page 98). See
Embroidery Stitches (page 18)
for stitch instructions.

1. Couched grid

STITCH NOTES. Stitch the
grid in 12-weight wool
thread, using one color for all
stitches in one direction and
a second color for stitches
made in the opposite direction. Make Couching Stitches
in embroidery floss; only the
center intersections have been
couched.

GERANIUM

Style Notes

Exterior: Bella Solids in Eggplant · Lining: Essex Yarn Dyed linen in Steel · Embroidery floss: Purple

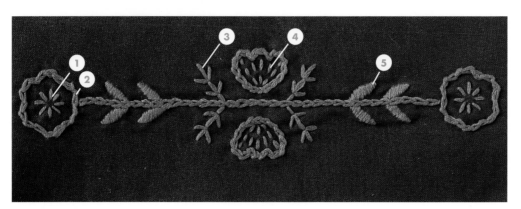

Stitch Guide

See pattern (page 99). See Embroidery Stitches (page 18) for stitch instructions.

1. Straight Stitch

2. Chain Stitch

3. Fern Stitch

4. Running Stitch

5. Satin Stitch

GRANNY SQUARE

Style Notes

Exterior: Essex Yarn Dyed linen in Black • Lining: Essex Yarn Dyed Metallic linen in Water • Embroidery floss: Blue, gold, coral, and light pink

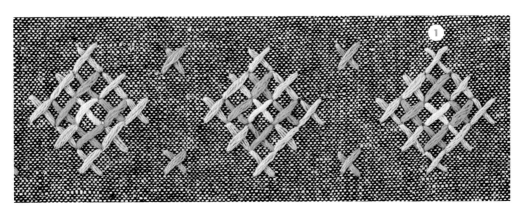

Stitch Guide

See pattern (page 99). See Embroidery Stitches (page 18) for stitch instructions.

1. Cross-Stitch

Sewing Directions

All seam allowances are ½″ unless otherwise noted.

PREPARATION

1. Remove the embroidered fabric from the hoop. Wash away any pattern marks or stabilizer; press. See Preparing Embroidered Fabric for Sewing (page 16).

2. Mark a horizontal line:

- 1″ above the embroidery for the Floret, Chevron, Geranium, or Granny Square patterns. Cut on the line. Use the same measurement for substitute patterns larger than 2″ in height.

or

- 1½″ above the embroidery for the Weave or Plaid patterns. Cut on the line. Use the same measurement for substitute patterns 2″ or smaller in height.

3. Find the center of the embroidery width-wise, and mark at the top and bottom edges within the seam allowance.

4. Position the Clutch pattern on the fabric, aligning the top edge with the fabric and matching the center marks.

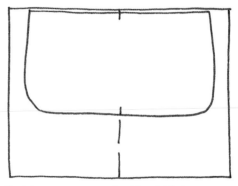

Position pattern on embroidered fabric.

5. Pin. Draw around the pattern and cut out the fabric.

6. Fuse the woven interfacing to the wrong side of the clutch's front and back. Position the fusible fleece on top of the interfacing, ¼″ from the top edge of the fabric and ½″ from the side and bottom edges. Fuse in place.

TABS

1. Trim the zipper to ⅜″ past the end stops (see Trimming Zippers, page 55). The total length of the zipper tape should be 8¾″.

2. Prepare and sew the zipper tabs to each short end of the zipper (see Sewing Zipper End Tabs, page 55).

DARTS

1. Cut out the darts on both the exterior and lining pieces.

2. Working on one dart at a time, bring the dart edges right sides together and pin. Sew the dart using a ¼˝ seam allowance.

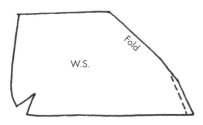

3. Repeat Step 2 for all 8 darts.

4. Press the seam allowance toward the outer edges on 1 exterior and 1 lining piece. Press the seam allowance toward the center on the remaining 2 pieces.

Press dart seams outward on one exterior and one lining.

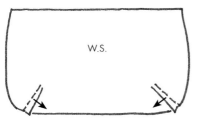

Press dart seams toward center on remaining exterior and lining.

CLUTCH ASSEMBLY

1. Sew the zipper to the exterior and lining fabrics (see Sewing Zippers, page 56).

2. Open the zipper halfway. Place the exteriors right sides together and the linings right sides together.

3. Push the zipper and tabs toward the lining. Align the zipper seams and pin (see Aligning Zipper Seams, page 57).

4. Align and pin the dart seams. Pin and sew around the side and bottom edges of the pieces, leaving a 6˝ gap in the lining's bottom seam.

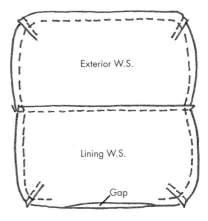

5. Press the seam open and clip into the curved bottom corners. Turn right side out; press.

6. Sew the gap closed by hand or machine (see Sewing the Gap Closed, page 59).

7. *Optional:* Thread the leather strip through the zipper pull to finish.

Patterns

Optional: Download and print Floret, Weave, Chevron, Plaid, Geranium, or Granny Square *and* Clutch A and Clutch B (see Using Patterns, page 13).

Floret

Weave

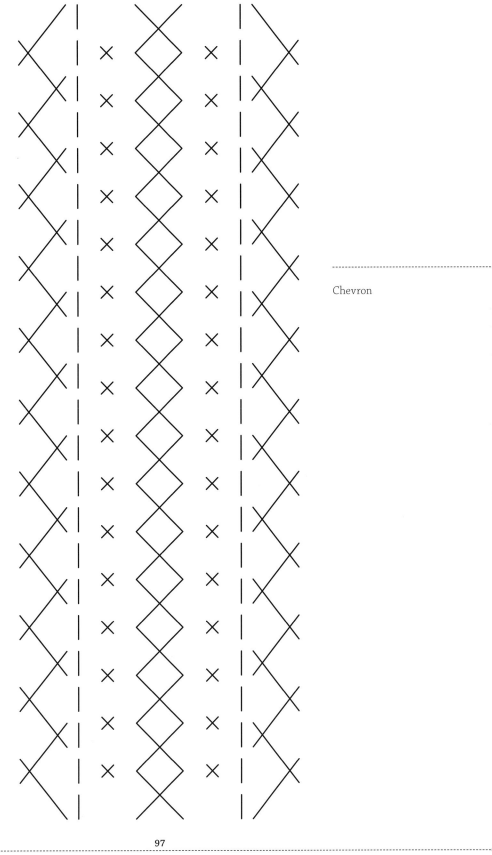

Chevron

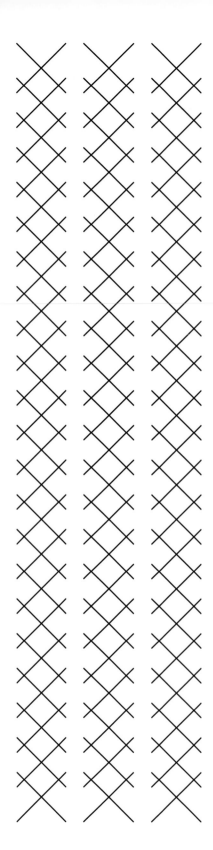

Plaid

A. Geranium

B. Granny Square

Clutch A

Center

Clutch A

Cut 1 *embroidered* exterior.
Cut 1 exterior.
Cut 2 lining.
Cut 2 woven interfacing.
Cut 2 fusible fleece.

Dart

Center

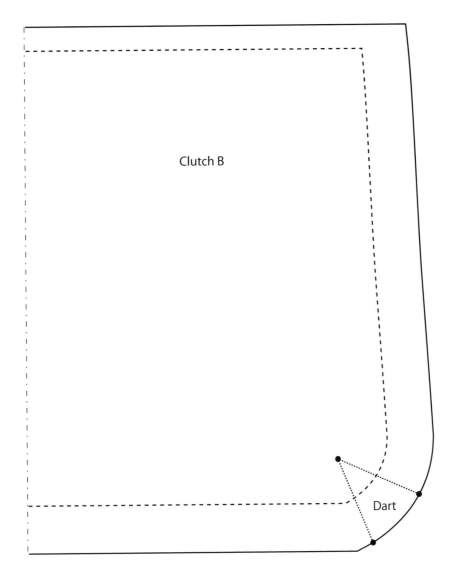

Clutch B

Dart

Finished flex case: 4½″ wide × 8″ high × ⅜″ deep

Flex Case

MATERIALS

Exterior: 1 fat quarter of yarn-dyed linen, fine-ribbed corduroy, Shetland flannel, or canvas

Lining: 1 fat quarter of yarn-dyed linen, quilting cotton, flannel, or fine-ribbed corduroy

Channel: 1 fat eighth of yarn-dyed linen (or yarn-dyed metallic linen), fine-ribbed corduroy, or lawn

Batting: 1 square 10″ × 10″

Fusible tape (⅜″ wide): 1½ yards, such as Clover fusible web (#4032)

Embroidery floss

Embroidery hoop: 6″

Flex frame: 4¾″ wide

TIP

To use a 4½″-wide flex frame instead, cut the 2 channel fabric strips at 5⅞″ × 2½″.

CUTTING

Exterior

• Cut 1 rectangle 8″ × 10″ for the front.

• Cut 1 rectangle 5¾″ × 8½″ for the back.

Lining

• Cut 2 rectangles 5¾″ × 8½″.

Channel

• Cut 2 strips 6⅛″ × 2½″.

Batting

• Cut 2 rectangles 4¾″ × 7½″.

Embroidery

Choose one of the six embroidery options (pages 104–109) to stitch on the case's exterior front. You could also choose to stitch a pattern from another project instead—just make sure it is 4″ × 6½″ or smaller in size.

1. Position the case's front with the short edges at the top and bottom.

2. Transfer the chosen design to the center of the front. See Positioning the Pattern (page 13) and Transferring Patterns (page 14).

3. Fix the fabric in the hoop. Stitch the embroidery as you wish, or follow the stitch instruction details on the photo.

DAISY

Style Notes

Exterior: Canvas • Lining: Essex Yarn Dyed linen in Steel • Channel: Cambridge cotton lawn in Nude • Embroidery floss: Pink, dark orange, orange, gold, green, and dark green • 12-weight wool thread: Coral

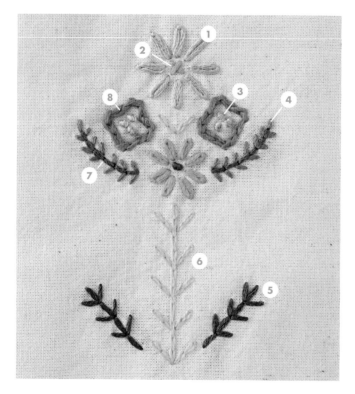

Stitch Guide

See pattern (page 113). See Embroidery Stitches (page 18) for stitch instructions.

1. Lazy Daisy

2. Cross-Stitch

3. French Knot

4. Straight Stitch

5. Fern Stitch

6. Chain Stitch (12-weight wool)

7. Backstitch

8. Chain Stitch

JUNE

Style Notes

Exterior: Essex Yarn Dyed linen in Aqua • Lining: Essex Yarn Dyed linen in Steel • Channel: Essex Yarn Dyed Metallic linen in Midnight • Embroidery floss: Light pink, orange, blue, and gold

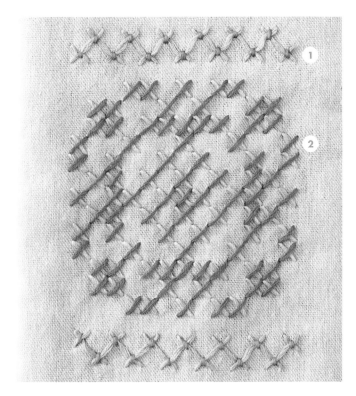

Stitch Guide

See pattern (page 113). See Embroidery Stitches (page 18) for stitch instructions.

1. Couched Herringbone Stitch

2. Cross-Stitch (multicolor stitches)

STITCH NOTES. Work each Cross-Stitch in two colors. See Multicolor Stitches (page 33). For Couched Herringbone Stitch, see Couching Combinations (page 32).

PETAL

Style Notes

Exterior: Essex Yarn Dyed linen in Charcoal • Lining: Flannel • Channel: Corduroy 21 Wale in Pink • Embroidery floss: Light pink, green, forest green, gold, orange, and green gold

Stitch Guide

See pattern (page 114). See Embroidery Stitches (page 18) for stitch instructions.

1. Van Dyke Stitch

2. Fishbone Stitch

MARGUERITE

Style Notes

Exterior: Shetland Flannel in Grey • Lining: Corduroy 21 Wale in Leaf • Channel: Essex Yarn Dyed linen in Berry • Embroidery floss: Medium pink, light pink, pale pink, gold, yellow, orange, green, and pale blue

Stitch Guide

See pattern (page 114).
See Embroidery Stitches (page 18)
for stitch instructions.

1. Cross-Stitch

2. Straight Stitch

3. Lazy Daisy

4. French Knot

5. Fern Stitch

HERRINGBONE

Style Notes

Exterior: Corduroy 21 Wale in Leaf • Lining: Quilting cotton • Channel: Essex Yarn Dyed linen in Aqua • Embroidery floss: Orange, medium pink, light pink, pale pink, forest green, medium green, and pale blue

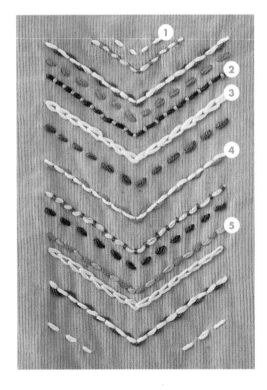

Stitch Guide

See pattern (page 115). See Embroidery Stitches (page 18) for stitch instructions.

1. Running Stitch

2. Couching Stitch

3. Chain Stitch

4. Laced Backstitch

5. Double Running Stitch

STITCH NOTES. See also Laced Backstitch (page 34). For double Running Stitch, see Double Stitches (page 33).

STARRY

Style Notes

Exterior: Essex Yarn Dyed linen in Steel · Lining: Quilting cotton · Channel: Cambridge cotton lawn in Gold · Embroidery floss: Medium pink, light pink, brown, dark brown, beige brown, gold, and white

Stitch Guide

See pattern (page 115). See Embroidery Stitches (page 18) for stitch instructions.

1. Lazy Daisy

2. Straight Stitch

Sewing Directions

All seam allowances are ½″ unless otherwise noted.

PREPARATION

1. Remove the embroidered fabric from the hoop. Wash away any pattern marks or stabilizer; press. See Preparing Embroidered Fabric for Sewing (page 16).

2. Trim the embroidered fabric to 5¾″ × 8½″, keeping the embroidery centered.

CHANNEL

1. Fold both short edges of the channel strips ⅜″ to the wrong side; press. Fold each side in ⅜″ again and press.

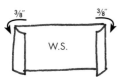

Fold short ends to wrong side.

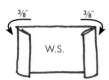

Fold short ends again.

2. Topstitch a scant ⅜″ from the short edges to secure. The finished width of the channel strips should be 4½″ or less.

Topstitch along short ends.

3. Fold the strips in half widthwise with the wrong sides together; press.

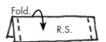

Finished channel strip

EXTERIOR

1. Cut lengths of fusible tape. Using the tape, center and attach the batting to the wrong side of both exterior pieces (see Using Fusible Tape, page 55).

2. Start with the exterior front right side up. Place one of the folded channel strips centered at the top edge. Align the raw edges, pin, and machine baste. Repeat with the exterior back and second channel strip.

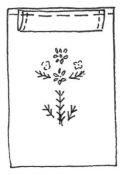

Baste channel to exterior.

CASE ASSEMBLY

1. Place 1 exterior and 1 lining right sides together. Pin and sew along the top edge. Repeat with the remaining exterior and lining.

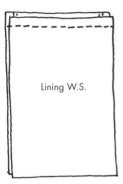

Sew exterior and lining together.

2. With right sides facing up, press the channels on each section toward the lining.

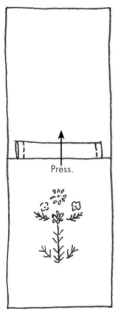

Press channel toward lining.

3. With the wrong sides facing up, press the seams open.

4. Place the 2 sections right sides together, with the exteriors facing each other and the linings facing each other.

5. Match the open seams at each side and pin. Pin around the remainder of the case.

TIP

Use fork pins to secure the open seams and help align them neatly (see Aligning Crossing Seams, page 58).

6. Sew all around the edge, leaving a 4″ gap at the bottom of the lining.

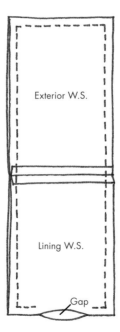

7. Press the seam open and trim the bottom corners. Turn right side out; press. Sew the gap closed (see Sewing the Gap Closed, page 59).

8. Insert the flex frame through the channel. Slide 1 metal strip through each channel, and bring the short ends out the other side.

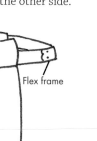

Flex frame

9. Bring the 2 sides of the open hinge together and insert the pin.

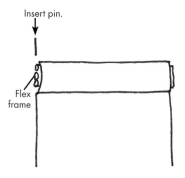

Insert pin.

Flex frame

10. Using pliers, fold the little metal flap at the top of the open hinge down to secure the pin in place.

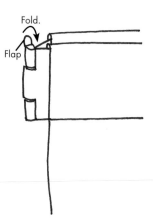

Fold.

Flap

Patterns

Optional: Download and print Daisy, June, Petal, Marguerite, Herringbone, or Starry (see Using Patterns, page 13).

A. June

B. Daisy

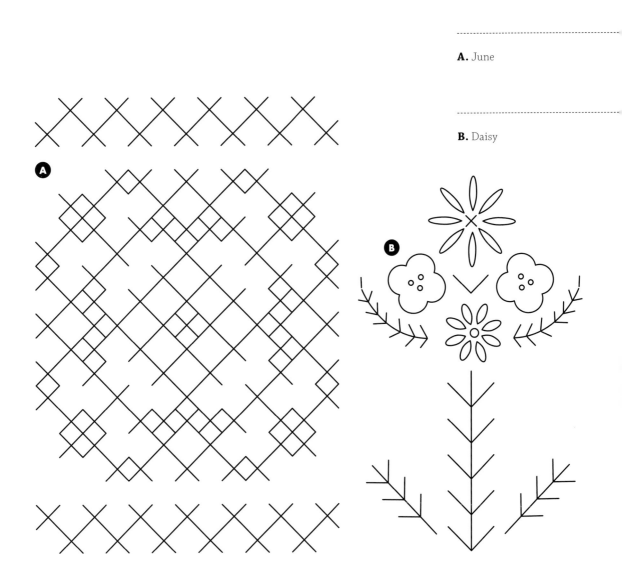

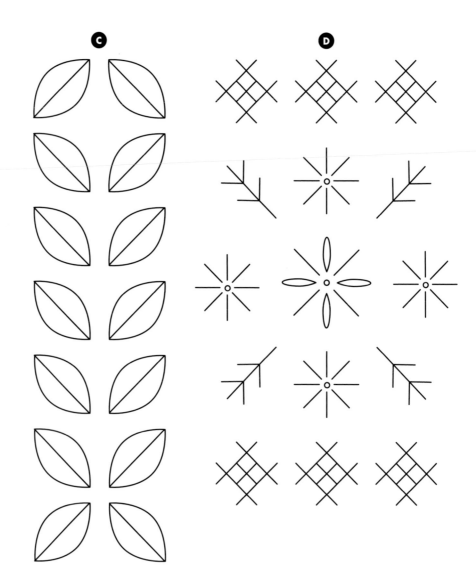

E. Herringbone

F. Starry

Small Change Purse

MATERIALS

Exterior: 1 fat eighth of yarn-dyed linen, yarn-dyed metallic linen, or cotton

Lining: 1 fat eighth of fine-ribbed corduroy, yarn-dyed linen, or yarn-dyed metallic linen

Zipper: 4″

Fabric glue stick, such as the Clover Fabric Adhesive Stick (#514), for attaching zipper tabs

Leather: ³⁄₁₆″ × 3½″ for zipper pull (*optional*)

Embroidery floss

Embroidery hoop: 5″

CUTTING

Exterior

• Cut 1 square 7″ × 7″ for the front.

• Cut 1 rectangle 6″ × 4″ for the back.

• Cut 2 rectangles 1½″ × 1″ for the zipper tabs.

Lining

• Cut 2 rectangles 6″ × 4″ for the lining.

TIP

When using a light-color quilting cotton for your exterior fabric, make sure to pick a light-color lining also, as a darker color may show through. Alternatively, fuse pieces of woven interfacing (cut to the same size) to the exterior pieces before sewing.

Embroidery

Choose one of the six embroidery options (pages 118–123) to stitch on the change purse's exterior front. You could also choose to stitch a pattern from another project instead—just make sure it is 4″ × 2½″ or smaller in size.

1. Position the change purse's front with the long edges at the top and bottom.

2. Transfer the chosen design to the center of the front. See Positioning the Pattern (page 13) and Transferring Patterns (page 14).

3. Fix the fabric in the hoop. Stitch the embroidery as you wish, or follow the stitch instruction details on the photo.

Small Change Purse

POSY

Style Notes

Exterior: Essex Yarn Dyed linen in Black • Lining: Corduroy 21 Wale in Pink • Embroidery floss: Bright orange, green, light green, gray green, light gray, coral, light coral, medium pink, and pale pink

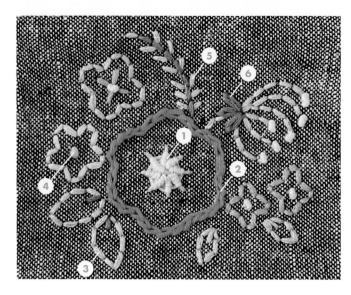

Stitch Guide

See pattern (page 125). See Embroidery Stitches (page 18) for stitch instructions.

1. Spider Web

2. Chain Stitch

3. Backstitch

4. French Knot

5. Straight Stitch

6. Lazy Daisy

CRISS CROSS

Style Notes

Exterior: Bella Solids in Pale Pink • Lining: Essex Yarn Dyed linen in Aqua • Embroidery floss: Light pink, orange, and navy blue

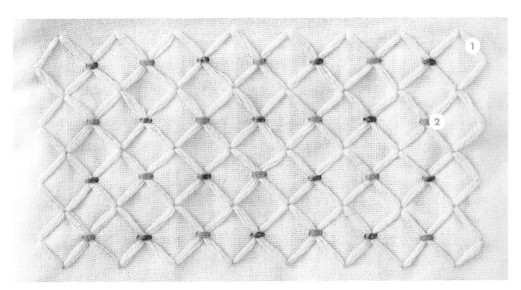

Stitch Guide

See pattern (page 125). See Embroidery Stitches (page 18) for stitch instructions.

1. Backstitch

2. Couched Cross-Stitch

STITCH NOTES. For the Couched Cross-Stitch, see Couching Combinations (page 32). Backstitch at the left-hand side using eight stitches in a zigzag formation. Repeat on the right-hand side.

BOUQUET

Style Notes

Exterior: Essex Yarn Dyed linen in Steel · Lining: Essex Yarn Dyed Metallic linen in Black · Embroidery floss: Medium purple, dark purple, orange, pale pink, and dark green

Stitch Guide

See pattern (page 126). See Embroidery Stitches (page 18) for stitch instructions.

1. Fishbone Stitch

2. Satin Stitch

3. French Knot

TRAVELER

Style Notes

Exterior: Essex Yarn Dyed linen in Espresso • Lining: Essex Yarn Dyed linen in Black • Embroidery floss: Pale pink, light purple, and dark purple

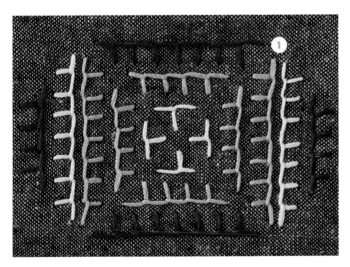

Stitch Guide

See pattern (page 126). See Embroidery Stitches (page 18) for stitch instructions.

1. Blanket Stitch

SPARKLE

Style Notes

Exterior: Essex Yarn Dyed Metallic linen in Midnight • Lining: Essex Yarn Dyed linen in Berry • Embroidery floss: Orange, light orange, medium pink, yellow, and pale blue

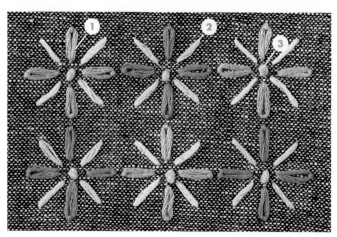

Stitch Guide

See pattern (page 127). See Embroidery Stitches (page 18) for stitch instructions.

1. Lazy Daisy

2. Straight Stitch

3. French Knot

PRIMROSE

Style Notes

Exterior: Essex Yarn Dyed linen in Peacock · Lining: Essex Yarn Dyed Metallic linen in Water · Embroidery floss: Bright yellow, pale orange, light gray, and green gold

Stitch Guide

See pattern (page 127). See Embroidery Stitches (page 18) for stitch instructions.

1. Chain Stitch

2. Lazy Daisy

3. Straight Stitch

4. French Knot

5. Herringbone Stitch

Sewing Directions

All seam allowances are ½″ unless otherwise noted.

PREPARATION

1. Remove the embroidered fabric from the hoop. Wash away any pattern marks or stabilizer; press. See Preparing Embroidered Fabric for Sewing (page 16).

2. Trim the embroidered fabric to 6″ × 4″, keeping the embroidery centered.

TABS

1. Trim the zipper to ⅜″ past the end stops (see Trimming Zippers, page 55). The total length of the zipper tape should be 4¾″.

2. Prepare and sew the zipper tabs to each short end of the zipper (see Sewing Zipper End Tabs, page 55).

PURSE ASSEMBLY

1. Sew the zipper to the exterior and lining fabrics (see Sewing Zippers, page 56).

2. Open the zipper halfway. Place the exteriors right sides together and the linings right sides together.

3. Push the zipper and tabs toward the lining. Align the zipper seams and pin (see Aligning Zipper Seams, page 57).

4. Pin and sew around the side and bottom edges of the pieces, leaving a 4″ gap in the lining's bottom seam.

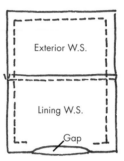

5. Press the seam open and trim the corners. Turn right side out; press.

6. Sew the gap closed by hand or machine (see Sewing the Gap Closed, page 59).

7. *Optional:* Thread the leather strip through the zipper pull to finish.

Patterns

Optional: Download and print Posy, Criss Cross, Bouquet, Traveler, Sparkle, or Primrose (see Using Patterns, page 13).

A. Posy

B. Criss Cross

C. Bouquet

D. Traveler

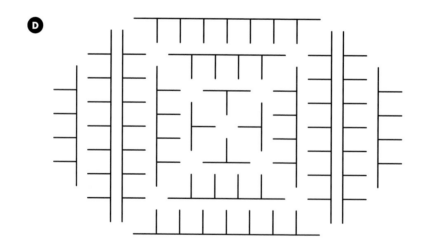

E

E. Sparkle

F. Primrose

F

Finished zipper pouch: 9″ wide × 6″ high × 1¾″ deep

Zipper Pouch

MATERIALS

Exterior: ⅜ yard of yarn-dyed linen or quilting cotton

Lining: ⅜ yard of quilting cotton, yarn-dyed metallic linen, or fine-ribbed corduroy

Woven fusible interfacing (20″ wide): ¼ yard

Low-loft fusible fleece (45″ wide): ¼ yard

Leather: ³⁄₁₆″ × 4½″ for zipper pull (*optional*)

Zipper: 8″

Fabric glue stick, such as the Clover Fabric Adhesive Stick (#514), for attaching zipper tabs

Embroidery floss

Embroidery hoop: 8″

CUTTING

Exterior

- Cut 1 rectangle 11″ × 10″ for the front.
- Cut 1 rectangle 10″ × 7″ for the back.
- Cut 2 rectangles 1½″ × 1″ for the zipper tabs.

Lining

- Cut 2 rectangles 10″ × 7″.

Woven interfacing

- Cut 2 rectangles 10″ × 7″.

Fusible fleece

- Cut 2 rectangles 9″ × 6¼″.

Embroidery

Choose one of the six embroidery options (pages 130–135) to stitch on the pouch's exterior front. You could also choose to stitch a pattern from another project instead—just make sure it is 8″ × 4″ or smaller in size.

1. Position the pouch's front with the long edges at the top and bottom.

2. Transfer the chosen design 2½″ down from the top edge and centered across the width. See Positioning the Pattern (page 13) and Transferring Patterns (page 14).

3. Fix the fabric in the hoop. Stitch the embroidery as you wish, or follow the stitch instruction details on the photo.

VIGNETTE

Style Notes

Exterior: Essex Yarn Dyed linen in Charcoal • Lining: Quilting cotton • Embroidery floss: Dark purple, medium purple, light purple, orange, and light gray

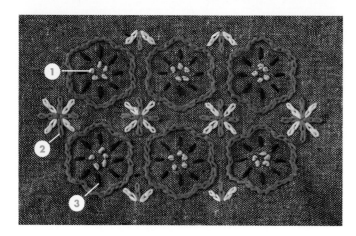

Stitch Guide

See pattern (page 138). See Embroidery Stitches (page 18) for stitch instructions.

1. French Knot

2. Chain Stitch

3. Straight Stitch

MARSEILLE

Style Notes

Exterior: Essex Yarn Dyed Linen in Steel • Lining: Essex Yarn Dyed Metallic linen in Dusty Rose • 12-weight wool thread: Navy, green gold, pink, green, gold, pale pink, brown, and orange

Stitch Guide

See pattern (page 139). See Embroidery Stitches (page 18) for stitch instructions.

1. Cross-Stitch (12-weight wool)

STITCH NOTES. I would recommend using the printed stabilizer method when transferring this pattern to ensure a neat, accurate finish. See Printing on Stabilizer (page 15).

To use stranded floss instead of wool thread, separate and use two strands of floss.

CURVE

Style Notes

Exterior: Essex Yarn Dyed linen in Aqua · Lining: Essex Yarn Dyed Metallic linen in Midnight · Embroidery floss: Dark purple, medium purple, purple, pink, orange, light orange, brown, off-white, and light gray

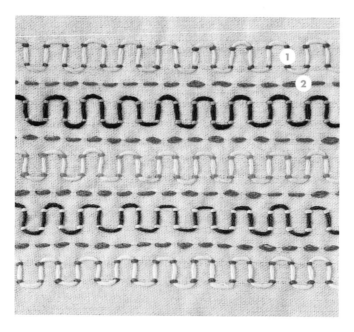

Stitch Guide

See pattern (page 140). See Embroidery Stitches (page 18) for stitch instructions.

1. Laced Running Stitch

2. Running Stitch

STITCH NOTES. See also Laced Running Stitch (page 34).

MARIGOLD

Style Notes

Exterior: Essex Yarn Dyed linen in Oyster • Lining: Corduroy 21 Wale in Leaf • Embroidery floss: Bright orange, medium pink, pale pink, gold, green, gold green, and yellow

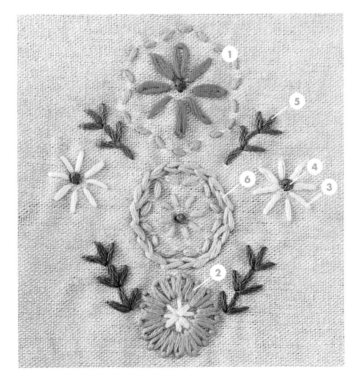

Stitch Guide

See pattern (page 141). See Embroidery Stitches (page 18) for stitch instructions.

1. Running Stitch

2. Lazy Daisy

3. Straight Stitch

4. French Knot

5. Fern Stitch

6. Chain Stitch

DAYDREAM

Style Notes

Exterior: Essex Yarn Dyed linen in Espresso · Lining: Quilting cotton · 12-weight wool thread: Bright pink, coral, dark purple, burnt orange, light pink, light gray, and gray green

Stitch Guide

See pattern (page 141). See Embroidery Stitches (page 18) for stitch instructions.

1. Satin Stitch
(12-weight wool)

STITCH NOTES. You also could use stranded floss instead of wool thread. Use two strands for the same fine detail or six strands for a slightly fuller look.

PIXEL

Style Notes

Exterior: Essex Yarn Dyed linen in Peacock · Lining: Quilting cotton · Embroidery floss: Coral, light coral, light gray, and medium pink

Stitch Guide

See pattern (page 142). See Embroidery Stitches (page 18) for stitch instructions.

1. Satin Stitch

2. Blanket Stitch

Sewing Directions

All seam allowances are ½″ unless otherwise noted.

PREPARATION

1. Remove the embroidered fabric from the hoop. Wash away any pattern marks or stabilizer; press. See Preparing Embroidered Fabric for Sewing (page 16).

2. Trim the front to 10″ × 7″, keeping the embroidery 1″ from the top edge and centered across the width.

3. Fuse the woven interfacing to the wrong side of both exterior pieces.

4. Draw and cut out a 1″ square from each bottom corner on all 6 pouch pieces: 2 exterior, 2 lining, and 2 fusible fleece.

5. Position the fusible fleece on the wrong side of each exterior piece, ¼″ from the top edge and ½″ from all other edges. Fuse in place using a pressing cloth.

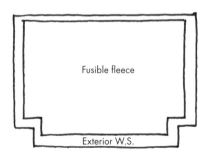

TABS

1. Trim the zipper to ⅜″ past the end stops (see Trimming Zippers, page 55). The total length of the zipper tape should be 8¾″.

2. Prepare and sew the zipper tabs to each short end of the zipper (see Sewing Zipper End Tabs, page 55).

POUCH ASSEMBLY

1. Sew the zipper to the exterior and lining fabrics (see Sewing Zippers, page 56).

2. Open the zipper halfway. Place the exteriors right sides together and the linings right sides together.

3. Push the zipper and tabs toward the lining. Align the zipper seams and pin (see Aligning Zipper Seams, page 57).

4. Pin and sew around the side and bottom edges of the pieces, leaving a 5″ gap in the lining's bottom seam.

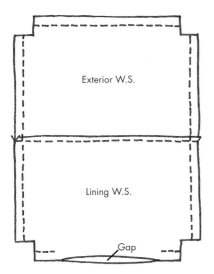

5. Press the seams open. At one of the bottom corners, bring the cut-out sides together, aligning the side and bottom seams at the center. Pin and sew to create a boxed corner. Repeat on all 4 cut-out corners.

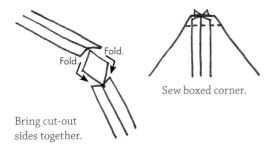

TIP

Use fork pins to align the side and bottom seams perfectly (see Aligning Crossing Seams, page 58).

6. Turn the pouch right side out; press. Sew the lining gap closed by hand or machine (see Sewing the Gap Closed, page 59).

TIP

To make it easier to press, insert folded-up batting inside the pouch to pad it out.

7. *Optional:* Thread the leather strip through the zipper pull to finish.

Patterns

Optional: Download and print Vignette, Marseille, Curve, Marigold, Daydream, or Pixel
(see Using Patterns, page 13).

Vignette

Marseille

Curve

A. Marigold

B. Daydream

Pixel

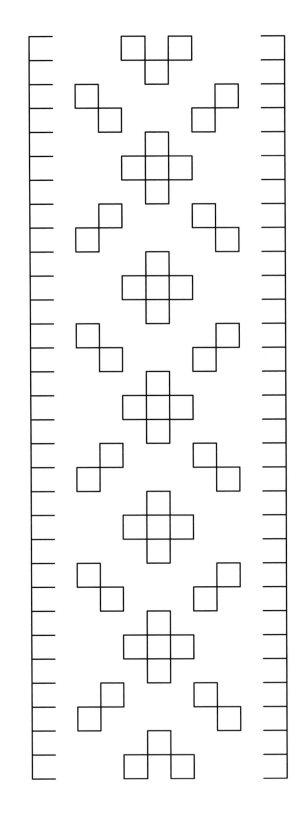

About the Author

Photo by Ciara Hoey

Aneela Hoey learned to embroider and sew in school at age eight and has been stitching up her ideas ever since. She studied printed textiles at Winchester School of Art and now designs prints for Cloud9 Fabrics, having previously designed several collections with Moda Fabrics. Aneela is addicted to both embroidery and making pouches, and she writes patterns for both, which she sells in her online shop.

Aneela authored the books *Little Stitches* and *Stitched Sewing Organizers* (both by Stash Books) and also had her work featured in *Aneela's Big Book of Pop Out Boxes* (by FunStitch Studio)—a title aimed at introducing creative youngsters to the idea of surface pattern and design.

Follow Aneela on social media

BLOG
comfortstitching.typepad.co.uk

PATTERN SHOP
payhip.com/comfortstitching

INSTAGRAM
@aneelahoey

Want even more creative content?

Make it,
snap it,
share it
using
#ctpublishing